Ex Libris

David J. Wrisley

While the late afternoon sun dries his freshly rinsed linen line, Zane Grey contemplates the day's fishing and composes notes from which a story will emerge. Big Mercury Island, New Zealand, 1929.

THE UNDISCOVERED
ZANE GREY
FISHING STORIES

Edited and with a Biographical Preface
and Background Vignettes by
George Reiger

Foreword by
James A. Michener

Winchester Press
an imprint of New Century Publishers, Inc.

Published in Association with
the Izaak Walton League of America

Printing Code

11   12   13   14   15   16

Library of Congress Cataloging in Publication Data

Grey, Zane, 1872-1939.
    The undiscovered Zane Grey fishing stories.
    1. Fishing stories.   I. Reiger, George, 1939–
    II. Title.
PS3513.R6545A6   1983   813'.52   83-17082
ISBN 0-8329-0316-7

Acknowledgments

I would like to thank Carol Dana, editor of *Outdoor America*; Mary Fuchs, volunteer librarian at the Ikes' headquarters in Arlington, Virginia; Jack Lorenz, executive director of the Izaak Walton League of America, who first conceived this project; and Robert Elman, editor-in-chief of Winchester Press, who saw how all the pieces would fit together. And, as always, special thanks to Barbara, my editorial assistant, typist, chief cook and bottle washer, and the mother of my 5-year-old buddy on bass fishing trips to the pond and tuna expeditions to the 20-Fathom Finger.

GEORGE REIGER

CONTENTS

Foreword by James A. Michener   ix

Preface by George Reiger   xiii

The Fisherman (introduction)   3

    The Fisherman Chapter I   7
    The Fisherman Chapter II   28
    The Fisherman Chapter III   34
    The Fisherman Chapter IV   42
    The Fisherman Chapter V   50
    The Fisherman Chapter VI   54
    The Fisherman Chapter VII   58
    The Fisherman Chapter VIII   64
    The Fisherman Chapter IX   72
    The Fisherman Chapter X   82

Sea Angling (introduction)   87

Sea Angling   89

Three Broadbill Swordfish (introduction)   99

Three Broadbill Swordfish   103

Permit (introduction)   111

Permit—A Rare Game Fish of the Coral Shoals   113

Birds of the Sea (introduction)   121

Birds of the Sea   123

The Seventh Wave (introduction)   127

The Seventh Wave   131

Trails Over the Glass Mountains (introduction)   141

Trails Over the Glass Mountains   145

Monty Price's Nightingale (introduction)   157

Monty Price's Nightingale   161

FOREWORD

by

James A. Michener

In the spring of 1924, when Zane Grey was one of the world's most popular and best paid writers, he handed the editors of the sporting magazine, *Outdoor America*, the manuscript of a novelette depicting a young boy's introduction to the world of fishing. He called it *The Fisherman* and would accept no money for having written it. Explained the editors, "The author has contributed this great serial as his part in the program to conserve something of the out-of-doors for the boys."

It is remarkable that this short novel has never appeared previously in a book. One would have thought that Zane Grey's name would have made it an immediate success, but apparently publishers feared it because it was so different from his traditional tales in western settings. Its brevity must also have worked against it. At any rate, it appeared in eleven installments, and it vanished after the Christmas issue of 1925.

It is well worth reprinting. Not only is it worthy of preservation as good Zane Grey writing, but it also tells a crisp, taut, nostalgic story of a boy's growing up in a simpler age. It is also a knowledgeable account of river fishing and takes its logical place among the more serious and substantial work in this field. It is certainly a legitimate part of the Zane Grey tradition—a part lost until now and worth preserving in book form. If there is a quaint or dated quality in this rediscovered work, it is an element of charm—the patina of age that glows from an authentic period setting.

We meet Lorry Dunn when he is four years old, pestering his mother about what fishing is. She replies succinctly, "A fisherman is a lazy bad boy grown up." We watch the lad's first perplexing experience with Old Muddy Miser, the fisherman who will play an archetypal role in Lorry's life. Finally, we watch as Lorry comes to know the river and its cherished spots: "There they sat eating and laughing, carefree for that day, under the magic spell of summer time at Dillon's Falls. Orioles and cardinals sang in the trees; swallows darted over the green water; song sparrows made sweet music in the willows. Then dominating all was the low roar of the falls. The sound entered Lorry's soul to swell there always."

There is no denying that the story itself is extremely old fashioned, with heavy-handed moralizing and sermons from Muddy Miser: "The bottle has had strange power over men of all races. There is only one other evil thing in life, lad, and that is woman. Bad woman! Perhaps I should say good woman made evil by men. There are fundamentally no bad women. They are the mothers of the race. But men are their enemies. You must have a noble ideal of womanhood."

Some of the plot is like that of a Zane Grey western, as when Lorry gets arrested in a local house of prostitution, where the girls seek to protect him with lugubrious results. But whenever Grey returns to the way Lorry slowly develops into a first-class fisherman, this simple tale rings beautifully true.

He does not catch the largest bass ever seen on the river. He engages in no special heroics. He learns slowly, makes many mistakes, and gradually comes to understand what fishing is.

It is a tale from another era when simpler values and more traditional forms of speech prevailed. Lorry Dunn is a varied character, prudishly upright at times, a social pariah at others. His fumbling attempts at courtship in high school are laughable, his inability to straighten out his affairs, inexplicable. In today's world, any one of his problems would be resolved quickly, but it is precisely this description of an older world that is appealing.

The same appeal will be found in the other Zane Grey writings presented here—seven essays and stories which, like *The Fisherman*, appeared in the magazine of the Izaak Walton League but were never published elsewhere. Five of them are about fishing or about the sea. They are of special historical interest because they include accounts of Grey's pioneering explorations of new kinds of saltwater angling. All of them, whether about fishing or other fields of interest, exhibit the charm and excitement of Zane Grey's finest writing about the outdoors.

It was a happy thought to include in this volume some of the original illustrations that appeared with Grey's writings in *Outdoor America*. The paintings by Frank Stick and others lend a lovely 1920s character to the text and were originally featured as prominently as the stories.

Zane Grey's western novels have been reprinted again and again, while his writings about the outdoor life have been largely neglected in recent years. This book will reveal a great deal about the other half of Zane

Grey's life: his addiction to fishing whether in Tahiti or Nova Scotia, and his dedication to the outdoors.

JAMES A. MICHENER
Honorary President
The Izaak Walton League

PREFACE

by

George Reiger

Zane Grey lived the American Dream. Not only is his the classic story of rags to riches, but Grey rebelled against the career (dentistry) fate had imposed on him and by dint of ambition, hard work, and luck, wrote his way out of a spirit-dulling routine to pursue a pattern of conspicuous consumption envied by any adventurous boy.

He mapped wild rivers in Mexico and lassoed and captured mountain lions in the Grand Canyon. He hiked through Death Valley "to see what it must have been like for those who hadn't made it." He pioneered fly fishing for steelhead trout in the Pacific Northwest and popularized angling for bonefish and permit in the Florida Keys. He bought a three-masted schooner and explored the South Pacific, catching world record fishes and picking up parcels of land along the way as souvenirs. (Not many years ago Malcolm Forbes, a latter-day, young-at-heart publishing success, bought Zane Grey's old fishing camp in Tahiti.)

ZG as friends called him, seemed to have done nearly everything, yet he was never content. Subject to dark moods and riddled by jealousy, he imagined that the people he most wanted to impress looked down their noses at his middle-class origins and, later, at his new money. A large part of Zane Grey's life was devoted to manufacturing and maintaining a legend of Zane Grey, with the hope the myth would outlive the man.

The fabrications begin with his birth date. Biographical dictionaries and encyclopedias cite the year of his birth as 1875, because that is what the editors found in *Who's Who*. However, Zane Grey pretended he was three years younger than he really was because he wanted people to think he had achieved his writing success at an earlier age. He wanted people to believe he was younger than his inspirator, Owen Wister, when Wister wrote *The Virginian*.

Owen Wister was 42 when *The Virginian* was published in 1902; Zane

Grey was actually 43 when *The Lone Star Ranger* first appeared on the best-seller lists in 1915. By rolling his birth year back, ZG felt he had achieved a victory over Philadelphia's upper crust, whom Wister represented and whose patronization Grey had to endure while a student at the University of Pennsylvania.

This competition was confined entirely to ZG's own imagination. The right people have never been concerned with who was born *when*, but who was born to *whom*. Furthermore, Owen Wister never viewed frontier fiction as his exclusive domain. He was well aware there was a literary tradition even before James Fenimore Cooper began concocting stories about pathfinders and deerslayers. Wister had no illusions that he was breaking new ground.

Yet it was less Wister's success than his social life, especially his close friendship with Teddy Roosevelt, that Zane Grey envied most. ZG wanted to be a friend of Presidents more than anything in the world, and when that didn't happen, he tried to prove his life was every bit as glamorous as that of any President.

Ironically, Zane Grey's life *was* glamorous, yet he diminished the achievement of his expedition to Utah's Rainbow Bridge by boasting he was there months before Teddy Roosevelt's party reached that same newly discovered and immensely fashionable landmark. (Zane Grey even left his initials at the base of the stone arch to prove he'd been there.)

In the Autumn of 1919, when ZG claimed to have seen the last wild passenger pigeons in Arizona, after Teddy Roosevelt had been given credit for seeing the last wild flock in Virginia in May 1907, the birding fraternity only laughed at ZG's claim. For one thing, passenger pigeons were never found in Arizona. For another, the passenger pigeon had clearly been an endangered species in 1907 and was certainly extinct by 1919. (The last captive specimen died in the Cincinnati Zoo in 1914.) ZG had no birding credentials to make credible sightings of passenger pigeons. Once again the people Grey wanted to impress yawned and rolled over when the obstreperous Zane Grey marched into their well-heeled circles tooting on his tin horn and tapping on his toy drum.

Zane Grey's parents, Lewis and Josephine Gray, may have contributed to ZG's later pretentiousness by naming their second-born son, Pearl Zane Gray, in honor of the mourning color Queen Victoria selected to commemorate the tenth anniversary of her Prince Consort's death. Like the "boy named Sue," Pearl Gray grew up hating his name and fighting innumerable battles with schoolmates to convince them of his masculinity.

There were several early influences on Pearl Gray which were to affect the course of Zane Grey's life. First, although he despised his father's career as a part-time preacher and full-time dentist (and would one day change the spelling of his family name to disassociate himself from his progenitor—as well as to hint at more distinguished antecedents), young Gray often worked in his father's office, removing sets of false teeth from the vulcanizer and scrubbing off the plaster. Later, it was this familiarity with the mechanics of dentistry, and not its science, that helped Pearl Gray pass through dental school.

The second influence was his friendship with an indigent character known as Old Muddy Miser. The right-thinking folks of Zanesville, Ohio—where Pearl Gray was born and brought up—were contemptuous of this unemployed hermit who made money by selling some of the fish he caught and lived in an abandoned pot-shop on one of the tributaries of the Muskingum River. They told their children that if they didn't study, work hard, attend church, and honor their parents, they would end up as "good-for-nothings" like Muddy Miser. Pearl Gray idolized the man, insisting he was a philosopher who had fallen from high estate. In turn, Old Muddy Miser nutured a love for fishing and independence in young Gray.

The third major influence on Pearl Gray was his discovery that his mother was a direct descendant of Colonel Ebenezer Zane, the founder of Wheeling, West Virginia; soldier in the American Revolutionary Army; trail blazer of what became known as Zane's Trace across the future state of Ohio; and first resident of Zanesville.

According to family tradition, Indian blood flowed in the Zanes, and Pearl calculated that he was $\frac{1}{16}$ Indian. Although this inheritance was a source of pride to the young man—as though a trace of Indian blood automatically made him a better outdoorsman—after he visited the West and was exposed to its cultural bias against red men, he felt some ambiguity about the value of his Indian blood. Although he writes with great feeling of the spiritual strength of Indians in an account of his first visit to Rainbow Bridge, Gray finally decided that Indians were necessarily inferior to the Europeans (especially the Anglo-Saxons) because Indians had lost their struggle to retain control of the New World.

This may have been simplistic reasoning couched in superficial social Darwinism, but it echoes the feelings of a generation of Americans who put the profiles of Indians on coins, named sporting teams for them, even set the statue of an Indian on the peak of the nation's Capitol—while hunting down the last independent tribes and herding them onto reservations.

Pearl Gray loved to read, but he read little that was recommended to him by his parents or teachers. Instead the "true" adventures of Buffalo Bill, Wild Bill Hickok, Wyatt Earp, and Jesse James were much more to his liking. Although several writers catered to the rage for western material in the decades following the Civil War, probably the best known and most successful of these was Edward Zane Carroll Judson (1823-1886), better known as Ned Buntline.

Since Judson's real name sometimes appeared with his alias on the title pages of his books, Pearl Zane Gray would have been intrigued by the Zane family connection. Judson's father had written *The Sages and Heroes of the American Revolution* which Zane Grey later used in researching his own first book, *Betty Zane*. In addition, both Ned Buntline and Zane Grey were Easterners who made their fortunes by writing fiction based on their travels in the West. Just as Judson owned a favorite house known as "The Eagle's Nest" in the Catskills, Zane Grey purchased a thousand acres along the Delaware River on the eastern fringe of the Poconos, built a home, and did most of his best work there. Although ZG moved to California and eventually died there, his remains were returned to the little cemetery overlooking the Delaware at Lackawaxen, Pennsylvania.

Pearl's principal socially-approved recreation was baseball, and both he and his younger brother, Romer Carl, were members of the Capital Club team of the Columbus City League. At this period in American history, baseball was more than a national pastime, it was a national obsession. Any male old enough to throw a ball and swing a bat was expected not merely to follow the game, but to play it. If one village could field nine able-bodied men, the honor of the next village was at stake until it, too, could field a team. Each city had a bevy of semiprofessional teams which were often more popular than any of the national clubs, because semipro players were local boys known personally to many of the spectators and because semipro players were often very good.

Pearl Gray was an especially talented baseball player. He was a superb pitcher who perfected the curve ball earlier than most of his contemporaries. In addition, and unusual for a pitcher, he was a crack batter and adept base runner. In brief, he was a model player, and baseball gave Pearl Gray the chance to excel.

The spring after Gray's twentieth birthday, the Columbus Capitals played and defeated Ohio State University and then took on Dennison, the best college team in the state and one of the best in the Midwest. Pearl Gray learned that a scout from the University of Pennsylvania was in the stands that afternoon and, rising to the opportunity, Gray pitched his team to a 4 to 3 victory over Dennison. Although he eventually received several offers of athletic scholarships, he accepted Penn's because Penn was in the Ivy League and played more prestigious opponents than either the University of Michigan or Vanderbilt University. Pearl's father favored Penn because it had an excellent dental school.

Pearl Gray did not get along well in college. He was older than most of his classmates and he resented having to kowtow to upper classmen younger and less experienced than himself. He felt his association with the baseball team should exempt him from the rules and customs imposed on freshmen. When he was harried by sophomores, he did the unthinkable: he fought back. Although desperately short of money, he turned down a job waiting on tables in the university's athletic association dining room so that he wouldn't have to wait on teammates.

The academic side of his college life was even more painful. Pearl Gray had always been a mediocre student, but at Penn he found his lack of aptitude in math and science pronounced. Had he been at Penn on the merits of his academic work alone, Gray would not have graduated.

His poor academic showing had less to do with his native intelligence, which his record later indicates was more than adequate, than with his proud and defensive temperament, which made him the kind of student few teachers can inspire or even enjoy having in class. Only the histology professor, Robert Formad, saw any potential in Pearl Gray beneath the many sizable chips he carried on his shoulders, and thanks to the 99 percent average Pearl Gray earned in Dr. Formad's course, Gray's cumulative average was brought up to the passing level, enabling him to stay at Penn and play ball.

Pearl Gray never drank alcohol because of an ugly experience in his teens involving liquor and his older brother, Lewis Ellsworth. As an athlete in training, he never smoked. Besides his rejection of two of the more popular social habits of his generation, Gray was aloof and a loner by temperament. He played ball and he played it well. In his senior year he knocked in the crucial run against the University of Virginia to maintain his team's undefeated record against such notable opponents as the New York Giants. Except for weekend fishing, canoeing, and camping trips with one or both of his brothers, Gray had few friends and little college-oriented recreation besides baseball.

In 1896 he graduated and moved to New York City, where he opened an office at 117 West Twenty-first Street. Like many other freshly minted college graduates, Pearl Gray may have imagined that his diploma represented a metamorphosis, that people with money and influence would recognize his special qualities, and that opportunity would come knocking at his door. Reality is always less sanguine than romance, and Gray barely recruited enough patients to pay the first year's rent.

He tried to keep alive the flame of his former glory by playing ball for a team in East Orange, New Jersey. He chose this club over more convenient teams in Manhattan because of the prestige of the Orange Athletic Club. Its players were mostly former college stars, and it was considerable consolation for the proud but lonely young man to sit in his office late at night and read the local newspapers' descriptions of him: "Gray is probably the most valuable accession to the team this year." "Doc Gray is famous for making home runs when needed."

Gray's moods during the next several years drifted between disappointment and discontent. Even changing the spelling of his family name and hanging out a new shingle—"Dr. P. Zane Grey, D.D.S."— didn't seem to help. Although ZG finally acquired enough patients to establish separate living quarters from the office where he had worked, slept, and eaten his meals, he jeopardized this modest improvement in his standard of living by moving his office to 100 West Seventy-fourth Street.

Perhaps the new location appealed to him because it was more suburban and closer to the American Museum of Natural History, which was frequented by such sportsmen and celebrities as William T. Hornaday, George Bird Grinnell, and Theodore Roosevelt. Or, perhaps ZG was aggravated by one or more of his Twenty-first Street patients—a doctor's or dentist's most reliable patients are often his most demanding, and ZG was never one to suffer people he despised.

On the other hand, the move uptown may have been made for no other reason than that ZG wanted to be near a certain young lady.

ZG had met this particular girl on August 28, 1900, while canoeing on the Delaware with his younger brother, R. C. Lina Elise Roth was studying at the Normal School of the City of New York (later called Hunter College) with the intention of completing her degree at Columbia and becoming a teacher. Undoubtedly, the darkly handsome Zane Grey dazzled Dolly (as ZG called her) when he descended from his lofty heights to flirt with her.

For his part, ZG admired Dolly for her beauty, wit, and education. At first he treated her like a younger sister, which she temperamentally was, considering her 17 years of age to his 28. From their first meeting until their marriage five years later, Dolly and Zane Grey grew intimate by sharing his goal of escaping the dull work of dentistry. She later helped provide the money to make this escape, and he helped her to develop a

After Zane Grey moved to Manhattan and opened a dental office, he lived more for his escapes to a river than he had even when he was a boy growing up in Ohio. Here he is, not long after the turn of the century, fighting one of the monstrous smallmouth bass that inhabited the Delaware River near Lackawaxen, Pennsylvania.

new and more confident personality. While Zane Grey helped a young girl become a woman, Dolly Roth helped a brooding and resentful boy become a man.

About the time ZG met Dolly, he switched his recreational allegiance from East Orange, New Jersey, to Chappaqua, New York, where the Camp-Fire Club of America had been founded in 1897. This fraternity, comprised mostly of city-bred sportsmen, sought to duplicate the flavor of an Adirondack hunting and fishing camp in Westchester County. Although the membership list is still structured by the Social Register, membership has always been based on a man's ability to pass a series of rigorous tests of his camping, canoeing, and woodcraft skills. Furthermore, a member remained in good standing only so long as he continued to refine these skills.

Zane Grey used tricks he had learned from Old Muddy Miser on the Muskingum to catch amazing numbers of these now legendary four-, five-, and even six-pound Delaware smallmouths. His "ghillie" is his younger brother, R. C., who is wearing one of ZG's University of Pennsylvania baseball shirts.

Dan Beard, who would organize the Boy Scouts of America in 1910, and Ernest Thompson Seton, who founded the Woodcraft Indians in 1902 and became Beard's "chief scout" in 1910, were early members of the Camp-Fire Club, as were conservation leaders like Gifford Pinchot and Teddy Roosevelt. The latter joined when he was president of the New York City Board of Police Commissioners and maintained an active interest in club meetings and events even after he moved to the White House.

Of special importance to Zane Grey were members George O. Shields, editor and publisher of *Recreation* and the founder of the League of American Sportsmen; Robert H. Davis, an avid angler and editor of *Munsey's Magazine*; John P. Burkhard, one of the founders of *Field & Stream*; and Eltinge F. Warner, who bought *Field & Stream* in 1908 and made it the official publication of the Camp-Fire Club from November 1910 through September 1916.

In this never-before-published picture taken by R. C., we see Zane Grey steering in the stern of a canoe while his close friend, Alvah James, paddles in the bow. The two young men are negotiating some rapids on the unruly Delaware in early spring.

These men had far more experience than Grey, but even as he admired them for where they had been and what they had seen and done, they respected his energy and athletic prowess. One of the most important events at Camp-Fire was the annual canoe race, and in this, ZG excelled. His coordination and sense of balance allowed him to make quicker starts and more agile turns. Grey was able to put more shoulder into each paddle stroke by standing throughout the contest, rather than kneeling as most of his competitors did. Years later, after he had a hand in launching Paramount Studios, Zane Grey asked one of the company's cameramen to film him shooting the rapids on Oregon's Rogue River. Although ZG was at least 50 years old by the time these movies were made, the brittle and faded film shows a grinning Grey negotiating the violent white water while standing.

It is doubtful whether Zane Grey had given much thought to becoming a writer before joining the Camp-Fire Club. His earnest tales of outings along the Delaware appealed to Shields and Burkhard, and they encouraged him to write, as did Dolly Roth. ZG's first attempt appeared in the May 1902 issue of *Recreation* as "A Day on the Delaware." His second effort, "Camping Out," appeared the following February in *Field & Stream*.

ZG was paid ten dollars for the *Recreation* article and a similar amount for the *Field & Stream* piece. He spent half his money buying additional copies of both magazines and passing them out to patients at his office and acquaintances at Camp-Fire. About the same time "A Day on the Delaware" appeared on the newsstands, Owen Wister's *The Virginian* appeared in the bookstores. ZG read the book and admired it, and he envied the way it maintained its place on the best-seller list, month after month. For the first time in his life, Zane Grey saw an escape from dentistry.

Although ZG wrote several more stories and articles in the next three years, he could sell none of them. The growing pile of magazine rejection slips did not daunt him, for he thought he had already proved himself in that market. He knew that his freedom from drudgery could only be obtained by writing books. Selling occasional magazine pieces for ten dollars would only serve to reinforce his feelings of enslavement as a dentist.

In the spring of 1903 ZG emerged from the kitchen, where he did most of his early writing, with a novel which, he told Dolly, would do for his reputation what *The Virginian* had done and continued to do for Owen Wister. *Betty Zane* is about ZG's great-great-grandaunt who had carried gunpowder in her apron through a hail of bullets to save her brother's command during the Revolutionary War. ZG personally escorted the manuscript to the first four of a dozen publishers who looked at it, but after a while, he let the book make the rounds by messenger. There were no takers.

ZG plunged into one of his dark moods and brooded about fate's determination to keep him chained to a dental drill. The more pessimistically he talked about his future, the more optimistically Dolly Roth talked about his upcoming big break. She offered to publish *Betty Zane* herself. ZG was furious at the suggestion, but he finally agreed. He reasoned that Dolly was merely making him a loan against the book's future profits.

Today *Betty Zane* is a collector's item. No one knows precisely how many copies were printed; the only copies ever sold were pressed on patients by Zane Grey or placed in a few bookstores by Dolly. Their disappointment was tinged with triumph: at last Zane Grey was a published author. Although Dolly Roth never recovered her investment in *Betty Zane*, she had made a shrewd investment, just the same. The book established a pattern of production for most future books by Zane Grey: ZG did the writing while Dolly read, corrected, proofed each page, and then helped negotiate the next contract.

ZG's second book was also about the Zane family. This time Colonel Ebenezer's brother, Jonathan Zane, was the hero. ZG picked a more colorful title—provocative titles were one of the hallmarks of Zane Grey's fiction—and A. L. Burt & Company agreed to publish *The Spirit of the Border*, but without any advance on royalties.

By the spring of 1906, ZG had finished a third book. Although this novel is now famous, no publisher would touch *The Last Trail* because sales of *The Spirit of the Border* had languished. At this point, any other aspiring writer might have given up, but ZG had no choice but to forge ahead. He had married Dolly the previous November and terminated his dental practice. The newlyweds had moved to Lackawaxen, where they hoped his small savings and her modest inheritance would sustain them until their mutual faith in the American Dream paid dividends.

ZG knew he had the imagination and stamina to produce dozens of novels, but he felt he needed a new direction. He wanted inspiration from personal experiences instead of history books and vicarious adventures.

His opportunity for a new beginning came indirectly. All his life Zane Grey had relatively few friends except his brothers, his wife, and later his two sons. (He also had a daughter, but she shared little of his far-flung outdoor life.) Some people thought ZG was shy; others considered him arrogant. Zane Grey was never comfortable when meeting people, and his erratic moods tended to drive old acquaintances away.

An exception was his best friend at the Camp-Fire Club. Although seven years younger than ZG, Alvah D. James was already an established writer basing most of his articles and stories on an expedition he had made up the Amazon and across the Andes to the Pacific Ocean. James enjoyed the Greys, and he was amused and flattered by ZG's awe of his success and worldliness. When ZG and Dolly visited Manhattan, they frequently shared an evening at the theater with Alvah James, and he made several trips to Lackawaxen to fish with ZG.

According to legend, Alvah James was responsible for providing ZG with his first opportunity to visit the West. The official version has it that Alvah James took ZG to see some wildlife films presented by "Colonel" Charles Jesse "Buffalo" Jones, and while the rest of his audience sat politely, but unbelievingly, through the old man's ramblings, ZG experienced an epiphany. The potential of the Wild West as inspiration for a young novelist suddenly struck Zane Grey with enormous force. He followed the disillusioned and lonely old Jones back to his hotel room and persuaded him that a professional writer–photographer would be just what Jones needed to accomplish his goals. ZG presented Jones with a copy of *Betty Zane* to show he was a published author and promised to publicize Jones' efforts to preserve the Old West. Buffalo Jones is supposed to have struggled to his feet, clapped his hands on ZG's shoulders, and exclaimed, "By Gum, son, we'll do it together!"

This lovely tale is marred only by the facts. Buffalo Jones was a successful and respected farmer from Garden City, Kansas (a town he founded), and he owned a huge ranch in Arizona. He had hunted bison in the 1870s, but his sobriquet, "Buffalo," resulted from his later work to save this species from extinction. Jones had helped protect the remnant bison herd in Yellowstone National Park from poachers, and he had even enlarged it with animals from his own herd.

Jones believed that for the bison to have a meaningful role in America's future, it should be treated as a domestic range animal, featuring quality meat and hides. He crossbred bison with black Galloway cattle to produce a variant called "cattalo" which Jones hoped would incorporate the stamina of the bison with the tractable disposition and superior meat of cattle. Jones had come East to raise money to continue his breeding experiments.

The actual meeting between ZG and Buffalo Jones may have taken place at a reception before Jones's lecture at the American Museum of Natural History or at a Camp-Fire Club dinner given in Jones's honor. Alvah James may have introduced Zane Grey to Jones or George O. Shields may have done the honors, since Shields was a member of the Camp-Fire Club's executive committee and was familiar with ZG's aspirations. The outdoor world of those days was a close little group of pedigreed talents, and it makes sense that Zane Grey got his first opportunity to travel West by formal introduction rather than by nursing a disillusioned oldster in a back room of the Grand Hotel. Furthermore, Jones made it clear: Grey was to pay for his part of the expedition and stay out of Jones's way.

They made their trip in the spring of 1907. As far as Buffalo Jones was concerned, it was a profitable venture. He had raised some money in New York and during his absence his cattalo herd had grown by 20 animals, each worth $500. And although Jones invested in a new dog pack, he recovered the money and made a profit when he was paid $100 by zoos for each mountain lion the dogs treed and he managed to capture alive.

For Zane Grey, the trip was a dream come true. He spent his first painful days in the saddle, learned to throw a lariat, met his first Indians, hunted bears and mountain lions, and heard stories around the campfires that he would later convert into some of the most popular novels ever written about the West. Within 15 years of his first trip to Arizona, Zane Grey had become a symbol of this vast and ancient land settled by young and energetic people. His books were selling better than anything else in print except *The Holy Bible* and *McGuffey's Readers*. Zane Grey split annual incomes of hundreds of thousands of dollars with his wife and took his share to see and do the kinds of things he had been unable to see and do as a young man.

ZG made Buffalo Jones the hero of his next book, which he called *The Last of the Plainsmen*. The book appeared in 1908 and earned only $200 during the first twelve months after publication. It was a long way from being in the same league with *The Virginian*, which had still not faded from the best-seller lists. However, ZG was confident that his next book, a novel and not merely an adventure reminiscence, would do better.

It did. *The Heritage of the Desert* was serialized by *Popular Magazine* for $1,000 and published simultaneously in hardcover by Harper & Brothers. It eventually earned over half-a-million dollars. Much of its success was due to Dolly's suggestion that ZG not sell all-time rights to his books to movie producers. She urged him to lease each title for a maximum of seven years, then ZG could rent the same property to another movie producer, whether or not a film had been made during that time. *The Heritage of the Desert* was brought to the silver screen three different times, earning royalties on each occasion. Nearly one hundred feature-length films were made from forty-four Zane Grey novels, certainly a record for any author.

Zane Grey's next novel was his most famous if not his most successful.

It was certainly his most controversial. Although Zane Grey had created Mormon characters for *The Heritage of the Desert* and would write again about Mormons in *The Rainbow Trail*, his emotional stand against the outlawed Mormon practice of polygamy created special problems for *Riders of the Purple Sage.*

Despite the fact *Riders* introduces the strong, silent, and basically good gunfighter to Western fiction; despite the strength of its opening and closing chapters which contain some of the most compelling moments in Western literature, and despite the fact that every editor who read the manuscript recognized its genius and called it "powerful" or "great;" the book made the rounds for months without any takers.

Bob Davis of *Munsey's* had originally asked for the manuscript but he was told to hold off by his boss, Frank A. Munsey. Teddy Roosevelt had begun organizing his campaign against William Howard Taft, and Munsey, a major contributor to Roosevelt's Progressive Party, didn't want anything in his magazine which could in any way be used against Roosevelt. The Progressives were counting heavily on the Western voter and the Mormon Church represented a sizeable block of such votes.

ZG can be excused for occasionally thinking that the right people were all against him. He knew he had written his best book yet, and he refused to delete the "offensive" material, because the action in *Riders of the Purple Sage* hinged on the evils of polygamy. ZG took the book to publisher after publisher, but each new editor said that he personally liked the book, but that it wasn't right for his audience.

Eltinge F. Warner, publisher of *Field & Stream*, finally asked to see the manuscript. He liked the book and wanted to serialize it.

"Are you sure it's right for *Field & Stream?*" asked the amazed author.

"Anything this good is right for us!" replied the man who later founded *Smart Set* just to get H. L. Mencken and George Jean Nathan to work for him.

Harper & Brothers published *Riders of the Purple Sage* in hardcover and subsequently handled every western and adventure book ZG ever wrote. The family legend has it that ZG went over the head of Ripley Hitchcock, the editor-in-chief, to one of the owners of Harper's to get *Riders* published. However, it is doubtful ZG had that kind of influence in 1912. More likely Ripley Hitchcock decided Harper's could not afford to turn down *Riders of the Purple Sage* the second time it was offered to them.

Another legend has it that since Zane Grey was one of the principal pillars supporting Harper & Brothers during the Depression, the Greys visited the publishing house and negotiated an unheard of fifty percent royalty on all the books produced by Zane Grey, Incorporated.

The truth is that in 1920, as he was approaching the height of his fame, ZG managed to negotiate a contract giving him an unprecedented twenty percent royalty on all copies after the first 10,000 printed. During the Depression, however, neither Harper's nor Zane Grey had the leeway to do more than maintain their old relationship and pray for better economic conditions.

By 1924, Zane Grey was paying as much as $54,000 in annual federal income taxes. Particularly vexing to ZG was the fact that the Internal Revenue Service would not permit him to deduct any of the travel and entertainment expenses associated with his hunting and fishing trips to gather new material for books and movies. The situation became so oppressive that, in 1931, the Greys made a trip to Washington, D. C. to plead their case before senior officials of the IRS, to no avail. The only pleasant rebate from this journey occurred when ZG was invited to the White House to talk about fishing with Herbert Hoover, a fellow angler. For several hours Zane Grey realized one of his fondest ambitions: he was the friend of a President.

Another consolation was his association with the Izaak Walton League of America. Zane Grey thought that just as the Granges were helping farmers to gain respect and obtain better prices for their crops and unions were enabling laborers to earn better pay and improve working conditions, the League was rallying sportsmen throughout the nation to gain political influence for the interests of fish and wildlife. At the bottom of every page of the early issues of *Outdoor America* was repeated the reminder of Judge J. M. Dickinson: "Fish and game cannot vote."

ZG's association with the Ikes also enabled him to be linked with the shakers and makers of his day without having to attend meetings and become involved politically. By donating stories and articles to *Outdoor America*, his material appeared alongside reports by such respected authorities as bass expert James A. Henshall; ornithologist Frank M. Chapman; angler and diplomat Henry Van Dyke (whom the Ikes featured as "the only man who ever has fly fished on the River Jordan and the Sea of Gallilee"); E. W. Nelson, chief of the U. S. Biological Survey; and President Calvin Coolidge, an active angler who attended and spoke before the Ikes National Conference on Outdoor Recreation.

Perhaps Zane Grey's association with the League gave him the opportunity to repay someone who had helped advance ZG's reputation as an outdoor writer. As early as 1910, Zane Grey referred to his friendship with Will H. Dilg, future founding father of the Izaak Walton League, in a short story called "A Trout Fisherman's Inferno." In the story, ZG dreamed he had died and, like all anglers, he was sent to hell. There he discovers many of his friends, including Will Dilg who has to row eternally for another angler, catching fish after fish out of a small boat.

"Poor Dilg!" writes Grey. "What a master mind had divined the one greatest punishment for him! No Eighth Circle could hold a greater!"

Two years later, Will Dilg was embroiled in a controversy about the fighting qualities of largemouth and smallmouth bass. Mr. W. P. Corbett had written an outdoor magazine to suggest that, pound for pound, the smallmouth bass was superior to the largemouth as a game fish. Will Dilg replied that such a statement was nonsense and that the fighting qualities of any bass depended entirely on water temperature and other local environmental conditions. Largemouth and smallmouth bass taken from the same lake, argued Dilg, were identical in behavior at the end of a line and in taste after coming out of a frying pan.

Mr. Corbett replied that he had indeed taken largemouth and smallmouth bass from the same waters, and the smallmouth was unquestionably superior. Mr. Corbett made his rebuttal more sarcastic than his original letter and he referred to Florida largemouth as "flabby monsters," comparing them to carp. In another context, he mentioned having taken many smallmouth bass from the Delaware with fly tackle.

Suddenly, like a champion of insulted virtue, Zane Grey rode onto the stage. He was angered by any comparison between bass and carp and he was annoyed to find someone who pretended to know as much as he did about bass fishing on the Delaware. ZG was also fiercely loyal to the few bosom companions he had in life, and he charged into print to support Dilg's thesis and friendship. Ten years later, when the Izaak Walton League was being launched, ZG donated, as Will Dilg put it, "thousands of dollars worth of his writings to *Outdoor America* because his heart and soul is [*sic*] in the work the League is doing"—and because ZG could never refuse a friend.

Zane Grey not only lived the American Dream, his meteoric rise in the 1920s and his gradual decline through the 1930s, ending with his death on the eve of World War II, paralleled America's own evolution from naviete and extravagance in the 1920s to economic decline and political dissent in the 1930s.

The older ZG grew, the more cantankerous he became. He wrote tirades against young Americans' immorality, automobiles in the wilderness, the rape of the seas by commercial interests, and the decay of every standard of excellence. ZG never perceived his own role in converting wild America into campground chains for middle Americans. He was one of the first tourists of the wilderness, and he wrote enthusiastically about its wonders, urging his readers to get out to see and do what he had seen and done. They did.

But for all his public rhetoric on behalf of the common man, ZG felt he was above the common herd. When Arizona enacted game restrictions for the first time in 1930, the state refused ZG special permission to hunt out of season even though he was Arizona's most famous part-time resident. ZG was "grossly insulted." He pointed out that "in twelve years my whole bag of game has been five bears, three bucks and a few turkeys. I have written fifteen novels with Arizona background . . . [and] my many trips all over the state have cost me $100,000. So in every way I have not been an undesirable visitor."

ZG must have known that Arizona would not embarrass itself with an exception to its new game laws, especially after all the bad publicity Grey had generated on the subject. Perhaps Zane Grey was only seeking a dramatic way to make a break with his killing past. For some years previous, he had experienced increasingly ambiguous feelings about the killing part of hunting. He loved the chase, but he disliked the inevitable end. In 1930, he abandoned his lodge in the Tonto Basin and never hunted again.

Zane Grey's pride was his Achilles' heel in his relations with people. He loathed being laughed at, and he imagined that people who had never had to work for a living were snickering behind his back because, by golly, he did have to work for a living! However, the snickering had little to do with how he earned his living, but much to do with the reckless way in which he spent his money. For example, although ZG hated seeing cars on rural roads, he couldn't get enough of them in the cities. When a Pasadena Lincoln dealer called him to say that his new models were several inches longer than those he had the previous year, ZG went down to the show room, looked over two of the new cars, couldn't make up his mind between two colors, and therefore wrote a check for slightly over $10,000—buying both cars!

Zane Grey was an active member of the Catalina (Island) Tuna Club. He even built an adobe-style house overlooking Catalina harbor and stayed there for weeks on end when the fishing was good. In 1920 he caught the largest broadbill swordfish of the season. It weighed 418 pounds, and although not the world record, it was still a notable catch. Grey quickly became a nuisance around the club as he repeatedly re-counted the minute details of his battle. He was boyish and sometimes even charming in his enthusiasm, yet in the egotistical way of a child, he never considered that others might not be equally enthusiastic about his trophy catch—especially in the fiercely competitive atmosphere of the Catalina Tuna Club.

ZG described how he had rowed all the previous winter to keep in condition for just such a fight. He told how he had soaked his hands in salt water to toughen them against the challenge of a record fish. He bragged about how his big swordfish had not swallowed the hook and, hence, had been able to render a fairer accounting of itself than many other fish caught in Catalina. He relived the blood, sweat, and tears that went into the battle, up to the gaffing and final flourish at boatside. It got so bad that most Tuna Club members tried to avoid him, ducking down behind newspapers when he entered a room or excusing themselves to run imaginary errands when he sat down on the arms of their chairs.

During the summer of 1921, Mrs. Keith Spalding, who, despite her tiny stature, was one of the finest anglers ever associated with the Tuna Club, landed a 426-pound broadbill. That evening nearly every Tuna Club member lined up in the vestibule of the clubhouse to call Zane Grey's house on the hill. They gave him the business—asking how far he thought Mrs. Spalding had rowed the winter before, suggesting that ZG should try Jergen's Lotion rather than salt water for his hands, pointing out that Mrs. Spalding's fish had been hooked in a far less sensitive spot than even his own fish, and so forth.

Zane Grey blew his cool. He declared that Mrs. Spalding could not have landed such a big fish by herself. She must have had help.

That kind of angry comment was exactly what some club members had been waiting for. Ray R. Thomas, vice president of the club that year, notified Grey that he must apologize to Mrs. Spalding in writing or resign. ZG did both.

Zane Grey's petulance caused his circle of friends to shrink. He eventually found himself in the ludicrous position of having to pay people to go fishing with him. One of these relationships was especially pathetic. On a fishing trip to Nova Scotia in 1924, ZG had met a former British army captain and remittance man named Laurie Mitchell. While there, ZG caught a world-record bluefin tuna and acquired a three-masted schooner. Mitchell had held the previous tuna record, and he signed an affidavit confirming ZG's greater catch when skeptics in the United States began scoffing at the claim.

ZG liked Mitchell and, in 1925, took him along on his first New Zealand visit. Grey caught the first broadbill swordfish ever taken off New Zealand as well as a record 450-pound striped marlin and a record 111-pound yellowtail. Mitchell went one better by landing a 976-pound black marlin, up to that time the largest gamefish ever caught on rod and reel.

It is never good politics for a second-in-command to one-up his chief, and this may have presaged the change in the two men's relationship. Their disagreements came to a head in 1931 after Mitchell's remittances

THE UNDISCOVERED
ZANE GREY
FISHING STORIES

"THE FISHERMAN"

Introduction

Something went wrong with the writing of *The Fisherman*. When the first installment of the novella appeared, Will Dilg, as editor, wrote that "the entire English-speaking world is familiar with the name of Zane Grey, who is writing *The Fisherman*, which will run intermittently over a period of several years in *Outdoor America*. The story will be The Compleat Angler of America told as the life story of an American. A story of childhood and youth, of manhood and maturity, of mellowing age! In this story Zane Grey will give the world the meaning of the joy, the beauty, the thrill, the religion, the philosophy and the soul of angling."

This was one heck of a promise, and the promise was enhanced by the fact that one of the foremost outdoor artists of the day, Frank L. Stick, pledged to illustrate the entire project. Stick's contributions not only stopped after installment number nine, but the installments themselves got progressively brief and stopped well before the protagonist, Lorry Dunn, had even reached "manhood and maturity," much less "mellowing age."

Many circumstances now unknown might have halted the project. One possibility is that Zane Grey simply had too many other more lucrative irons in the fire. Or he might have become bored with the story of Lorry Dunn, although this is doubtful considering the autobiographical content of the work. Or the matter of censorship might have arisen after installment seven, in which young Lorry visits a whorehouse. A good many Ikes may have decided that "scantily clad . . . voluptuous" women with bare breasts had no proper place in the pages of *Outdoor America*. Whatever the reason, there is an unfinished quality to *The Fisherman*. Taken by itself, the story is complete. Yet taken in the context

Even after Zane Grey became obsessed with big game, he never lost his fascination for small streams such as this one, Mast Hope Brook, near his Pennsylvania home.

of its *Outdoor America* setting, there is the hint of something more that now will never be known.

It seems doubtful that ZG would have voluntarily abandoned his work on *The Fisherman* because it offered him an opportunity to indulge his autobiographical urge. The story of Lorry Dunn is a thinly disguised account of his own upbringing in Zanesville, whose name is changed here to "Hainsville." Lorry's family's name is Dunn, and it doesn't take too much imagination to compare the color *dun* as to his own family name *gray*. Lorry is short for Loren, the name of Zane Grey's younger son, and Lorry's younger brother, *Homer*, is close enough to Zane Grey's own younger brother, *Romer,* to imply that the writer worked from personal reminiscence.

In some cases, Zane Grey didn't bother to change names from his youth. The Tomans and Graves brothers have the very names they had in Zanesville. Similarly, both Pearl Gray and Lorry Dunn were born and reared in the Terrace section of Zanesville (Hainsville) and went to the Eighth Ward school. Dillon's Falls, Joe's Run, and other stream locations in the story are all genuine names in the Licking and Muskingum watersheds.

Thanks to a unpublished autobiography of Zane Grey covering all the years of *The Fisherman* and some beyond, we note some interesting differences between the lives of Lorry Dunn and Pearl Gray. A few are superficial. For example, the family next-door, with whom the Dunns picnic above Dillon's Falls, is named Linden in *The Fisherman.* In real life, they were the Lindsays. Other anecdotal details, however, are significantly different. For example, when young Pearl Gray first played the "pillow game," a girl named Margaret kissed him and then he kissed his neighbor, Daisy Lindsay. In *The Fisherman,* however, Lorry is kissed by a girl named Alice Fall who so overwhelms Lorry he dashes out of the party and runs home.

In Pearl Gray's life, the first girl he loved was named Alice Fell. He lost her one day at recess when proud and unable to admit defeat, he stole his marbles back from a boy named Bud Crub who had won them fairly in a match. Crub chased Gray inside the school and cornered him in a classroom. In desperation, Gray picked up a sponge heavy with water and ink. He hurled it at Crub, Bud ducked, and the sponge struck Alice Fell squarely in the breast, just as she innocently rounded the door of the classroom. Her new dress was ruined, and so was any future romance between Pearl Gray and Alice Fell. Thus, Zane Grey used the opportunity of *The Fisherman* to explore what might have been.

There is both pleasure and sorrow in reading *The Fisherman* in the context of the *Outdoor America* issues in which it first appeared. The pleasure lies in ZG's often lyrical portrayal of small-town life in rural America toward the end of the nineteenth century; a Currier & Ives print in prose. The sorrow is in the amazing optimism that once existed in our society concerning the quick victories to be achieved by conservationists leaving the reader to wonder at the naiveté of our fathers or to regret that such faith ever passed out of American life.

The editorial page of the July 1924 issue is devoted to celebrating the signing of a federal law, the Upper Mississippi Wild Life and Fish Refuge Act, that "makes safe forever 300 miles of the Mississippi River bottom extending from Rock Island, Illinois to Wabasha, Minnesota."

Will Dilg rhapsodized about the miracle that had been performed and that "the God of Nature and the wild places and wild things [had] WON." Zane Grey wrote to congratulate the League and to recommend that now we must "get together and gather weight until we are so mighty and powerful that we can save the woods and waters from despoilation, and awaken a spirit to save America for Americans." Icthyologist David Starr Jordan wrote to praise the League for saving the great breeding waters of native fishes in the Mississippi, and bass authority James Alexander Henshall wrote to "praise God from whom all blessings flow for the blessing of the Upper Mississippi Preserve."

Unfortunately, to many legislators, the word *forever* means only until the next election, and the Upper Mississippi Wild Life and Fish Refuge has long since gone the way of other noble dreams. The sad lesson in reading old issues of *Outdoor America* is that the price of a bountiful and healthy environment is eternal vigilance. That is the bitter but true meaning of the word *forever* in the context of conservation.

GWR

THE FISHERMAN*

by

Zane Grey

CHAPTER I

Lorry Dunn's mother complained to her neighbors that the boy was older than his years and growing very precocious. His fourth birthday happened in June; and around that time Lorry developed a propensity to run off and hide in the willows along Joe's Run and divest himself of all his clothing. He loved to be alone. Then, too, the amazing discovery was made that he was actually fond of water, if he could wade and dabble in it. But Lorry had a most strenuous objection to water in connection with soap and wash rag.

At length Mrs. Dunn resorted to an expedient common to all mothers of little boys.

"Lorry," she began severely. "Joe's Run is a bad place. Old Muddy Miser goes there, and he'll catch you if you don't watch out."

The name interested Lorry. He had heard it somewhere in a connection that was fascinating and fearful. But he had forgotten.

"Who's Old Muddy Miser?" he asked.

"He's a fisherman," replied his mother with great force, "a lazy good-for-nothing fisherman who lives at Dillon's Falls."

"What's a fisherman?" queried Lorry.

---

*ZG, like all anglers, was a superstitious man. He believed in omens. The month after this story first appeared in *Outdoor America*, Zane Grey caught in Nova Scotia the largest bluefin tuna ever taken on rod and reel, a 758-pounder, on August 22, 1924. This was an amazing angling feat, and considering the primitive big-game tackle of that time, it is a record which has never been beaten. Inspired by his good fortune, and while still in Nova Scotia, ZG bought a three-masted schooner in which he intended to fish all the southern seas. He named his new ship, *The Fisherman*.

Zane Grey was at the height of his fame and fortune when he wrote "The Fisherman" and bought and outfitted this three-masted schooner which he then rechristened *The Fisherman*.

The good woman perceived that here was an instance of Lorry's awakening intelligence and an opportunity to stamp upon it an image of the general unworthiness Lorry's father attached to all fishermen. Personally she had never seen anything harmful in fishing, except that it encouraged an idle disposition and a habit of sitting in the sun.

"Lorry, a fisherman is a lazy bad boy grown up." she said, cudgeling her brains for apt expression to impress this youngster. "He never helps his mother. He is dirty and disobedient. He plays hookey and won't work. Then when he gets to be a man, all he does is trudge off to Joe's Run or Licking Creek with a long fishing pole over his shoulder. He stays away all day and is never home for supper. Folks say a fisherman always carries a bottle with him. You've seen a drunken man; that's a fisherman."

"Uncle Jake Price gets drunk," replied Lorry. "But he never has a fissin' pole . . . Mama, what's fissin'?"

"Well, Lorry, it's a terrible waste of time," replied Mrs. Dunn, feeling that in the way of sincerity the matter was getting beyond her. But Lorry's hazel eyes were hard to resist. "You go way off to the brook in the woods or farther to the river. You have a long pole with a line tied to it, and a hook on the end of the line. You stick a worm on the hook and throw it in the water. Then you sit there holding the pole for ever so long."

"Mama, what happens when you do that?" queried Lorry.

"Why, sonny, if you're lucky you catch a fish," she said, wondering what made him so much more curious than usual.

"What's lucky?" he flashed up at her.

It turned out that Mrs. Dunn's limited knowledge of fish and fishing was greatly inadequate for the occasion. She feared that she had not at all given the unfavorable impression she knew would please the boy's father. On this particular subject Lorry exhibited an unabatable curiosity. He amazed her, too, by his babbling about the fish he had seen the rivermen carrying on a string, and on the shelves at the market.

"But, Mama, they were all dead," he averred with solemnity, as if that made a tremendous difference, which he felt but could not understand.

It was on a stage ride to Brownsville that Lorry saw his first real live fish. His mother was taking him to visit an aunt who lived in the country. Lorry had the joy of sitting beside the stage driver on the front seat. At the foot of a long hill the driver halted the horses. The July day was hot and the road furnished little shade.

A tiny stream of water came down the hillside, along the road, in some places making little pools. It so happened that Lorry from his high perch looked down into a clear pool directly beneath him. What he saw transfixed him with strange rapture. Against the sunlit amber depths of the little pool shone a wondrous fish creature that came to the surface and snapped up a bug. It flashed silver and rose. It had a green back covered with many black specks.

"Oh, what's that?" gasped Lorry, clutching the driver, and pointing down with quivering hand.

The good-natured man leaned over to direct his gaze at the place indicated.

"That's a chub,"[1] he replied. "Boy, you've sharp eyes."

"Chub!" exclaimed Lorry, under his breath. "Could I catch him?"

"Reckon so, if we had time. All you'd need would be a stick, a piece of cord, a bent pin, an' a grasshopper. But we must be climbin' the hill."

---

[1] Probably a creek chub (*Semotilus atromaculatus*) or a silver chub (*Hybopsis storeriana*). Although there were more than 45 species of minnows (Cyprinidae) represented in the largely undammed and unpolluted Ohio River watershed of the 1880s, the creek and silver chubs were and still are among the most common. Furthermore, their maximum sizes make them sporty fishes for youngsters. The silver chub grows to nearly nine inches long, and the creek chub grows to more than 12 inches.

Lorry leaned far back to hold the last glimpse of his first fish, and as the stage started he saw the chub dart into the shadow of the bank. He felt his rapture fade to a sickening sense of loss. No bird, no animal, no toy had ever roused the yearning so suddenly born for this shiny speckled little fish. Before the stage climbed to the summit of that long hill Lorry was a changed boy. The vagueness of childish dreams expanded into wonderful enchantments. The horses, the ride, the stage driver no longer excited his attention. He peered into the woods along the road, through the beech and oak trees, and on into the green obscurity with dreamy eyes haunted by a tiny brook.

Not long afterwards a second unforgettable event came to mark the tranquil course of Lorry's childhood. One day there was great excitement at his home on the Terrace and he was taken to play at Madden's Hill, a place of glamour consecrated to the elder boys. Upon his return he was told that he had a baby brother. At first Lorry was not thrilled, but he was curious. They let him see his mother and the queer little red-haired thing they said was the baby brother. Lorry felt concerned about his mother, she was so white and strange. But her smile seemed beautiful. Something swelled his heart.

"Lorry," his mother whispered, "you'll have a playmate now. His name is Homer."

"I'm glad it's no girl," he said, suddenly awakening to a new aspect of the case. Then he dared to peer closer at the wrinkled little mite his mother called Homer. A sense of ownership gathered round that strange deep oppression in his breast. Brother! The word lingered with him, long after they took him away. Soon he could have this brother to sleep with him in the dark room that for Lorry was always full of shadows of ghosts. Lorry had fear of the black night and that fear increased with him as the years passed. The terror of night and cold grew with Lorry's imagination.

Soon after Homer came, Lorry started to school in the old Eighth Ward schoolhouse, a square brick structure about which his elder brother Cedric told such wonderful stories. But nothing happened as Lorry imagined it would happen. He guessed he did not like school very well. The boys of the Eighth Ward did not think much of the Terrace boys. There was a class hatred as old as Hainsville. Lorry felt it without understanding what it was all about, and was most eager to let these boys know it did not matter to him. His overtures, however, were rewarded by a buffet on the nose—which outstanding event of his early school days checked his predisposition for the companionship of Eighth Ward boys.

While Lorry packed his books down the winding path over the hill and across the park, through snow and grass and autumn leaves, the years sped by apace. Homer attained the remarkable age of four. He was a chubby little rascal, round-faced and freckled, with red hair and large ears. He was so fat he could not climb halfway to the first branch of the maple tree in the yard. His many efforts, however, were commendable and encouraged Lorry to hopes.

Lorry had lived through ages waiting for the long vacations, and that one of his tenth year seemed never to come. The more he went to school the lengthier grew the days! Aside from the allurement of the longed-for vacation there was a promise from his father to take them a whole day to Dillon's Falls. That name was music to Lorry's ears. He did not know why. It was associated only with vague dreams, and stories he could not recall. He had never been there.

At last the great day dawned. Lorry had not slept much. He was wild for this adventure and bewildered Homer with his ravings. It was to be a picnic day. All the Dunns were going, and had invited a neighbor family, the Lindens, who, numerous as they were, had no member quite so young and small as Homer.

Armed with baskets of good things to eat, and fishing poles and sunshades, they set out to walk the three miles to Dillon's Falls. The July day, beautiful and rich with its golden light, was yet warm. The green woods looked so inviting that Lorry did not wonder at Homer for wanting to stop there. Beyond the woods the road wound down a hill to meadowland, where larks and blackbirds were singing, and a wandering line of willows marked the course of Joe's Run.

Lorry tarried on the wooden bridge that spanned the little stream and he peered down into the green water as it swirled under the drooping willows and glided on to a shallow place, to ripple and rush and murmur over yellow rocks. The color, the movement, the mystery charmed the lad, and seemed to find something calling in his soul. He longed to stay there, to wade in the water, to linger under an enormous elm tree that spread cool shade over grassy bank and dark pool. But he had been given the task of looking after his little brother, and remembering this he hurried on to catch up.

The road was dusty, the distance long, the sun hot. They passed the county poor house, and Lorry's father, a tall man with large nose and piercing eyes, teased Lorry by remarking if he did not do better in school he might end up there. Beyond this point there were shade trees, maples and walnuts, bordering the road and affording a most welcome change. Then they passed a little red schoolhouse set back in a grove, and Lorry thought he would much rather go there than to the prison-like Eighth Ward schoolhouse.

A little while after passing this place the discovery was made that Homer was missing. Lorry espied him sitting back along the roadside. It turned out that Homer was so tired he did not want to go any farther. Lorry persuaded and scolded in vain. Then he resorted to a means he well remembered.

"Old Muddy Miser will catch you if you don't watch out."

This admonition was effective. Homer had heard of this old demon of the river and he found strength to continue the journey, not, however, without holding Lorry's hand.

They fell behind the rest of the picnic party, and together turned down the dusty road and entered the covered bridge that crossed Licking River. The boards on the floor were loose; they rattled, and bumped up, threatening to stub the boys' bare toes. Here and there were holes in the wall; and finally, they came to a place where a board had been broken out. Lorry heard running water. Still holding to his little brother, Lorry peeped out. He saw green rushing water, clear over gravel bars, and huge gray rocks, and beautiful white-barked sycamore trees, and then a long lane of river broken by rifts and low falls and foamy rapids.

"Oh, Homer! Look! It's Dillon's Falls," cried Lorry.

That Homer looked long and had to be dragged away from the aperture argued well for Lorry's enthusiasm. They crossed the rattling bridge, out into the sunlight again, and ran the rest of the way down under shady elms and sycamores to where their father waited for them.

"Boys, this is Big Rock," he said, indicating the huge bank of gray stone that overhung the river. "Many a time I fished here with my Dad, when I was little."

"What'd you ketch?" queried Lorry, his eyes sparkling.

"Bass, catfish, and red-horse suckers[2]—sometimes half a wagonload," replied his father.

Thus began for Lorry and Homer the dawn of enchantment by running waters. They fished for hours with a hope and patience worthy of better fortune. Perhaps it was an augury of their future in that nothing was to come easy. Homer sat beside his brother and waited with a most marvelous optimism. But no fish took their wormy lures. They were called, presently, to the picnic dinner spread on the verdant grass under the broad-leaved sycamores. It was a joyous occasion. Lorry did not

---

[2] There are several species of redhorse sucker (*Moxostoma* sp.) found in Ohio. Some of these fish grow more than two feet long and attain weights up to ten pounds. Despite many small bones, they are excellent eating. Unfortunately, and despite their rugged common name, redhorse suckers are extremely susceptible to pollution and are usually the first to die in aquariums of native freshwater fishes if the water is at all impure. For this reason, redhorse sucker populations throughout mid-America are pale shadows of their former abundance.

realize it then, but that family group was etched on his memory forever. His father, with pale lined face, for once bright with pleasure; his mother, with her soft dove eyes and gentle smile; Cedric and Gertrude,[3] auburn-haired and handsome, bantering as usual after the manner of brothers and sisters; and last little Homer, with his round and freckled face, his shock of red hair, his chubby bare legs all scratched and muddy—there they sat eating and laughing, carefree for that day, under the magic spell of summer time at Dillon's Falls. Orioles and cardinals sang in the trees; swallows darted over the green water; song sparrows made sweet music in the willows. Then dominating all was the low roar of the falls. The sound entered Lorry's soul to dwell there always. This first visit to Dillon's Falls was like a dream come true.

In the afternoon the boys' father took them down off the high bank into the willows that lined the stream. Here he showed them huge balls of water snakes wrapped and tangled round low branches, their squirming fat brown bodies woven together, and innumerable heads and tails sticking out. Homer was frightened, but Lorry threw stones at the writhing balls and sent snakes gliding into the water.[4]

From there the boys went on to where the water grew shallow and waded out upon the wide rock bottom of the river. There were dry ledges and shelves of rock that led far out toward where the rushing white channels roared. A long low fall of water, pouring over a four foot drop into a foamy green stretch, held unaccountable fascination for Lorry. At the edges of the dry places there were deep smooth holes worn in the rock, full of clear water, and peopled by tadpoles and crawfish and tiny minnows. At once these aquariums claimed Homer, and manifestly he was more bent upon capture than an unconscious study of natural history. When he muddied one hole he passed on to another. Lorry was

[3]Although Lorry Dunn has three siblings, Pearl Gray had four: two sisters named Ella and Ida, and two brothers named Lewis Ellsworth and Romer Carl. Pearl thought his older brother's name, Ellsworth was stuffy. That's probably why Lorry's older brother is named Cedric; that's stuffy, too.

[4]This is the kind of anecdote that gets Zane Grey into trouble with naturalists who spend more time in laboratories than in the field. They protest that ZG's description of northern water snakes (*Natrix sipedon sipedon*), wrapped and tangled "in huge balls," is nonsense. They insist that while many species of snake show comparable behavior at permanent dens or on the eve of hibernation, no one in modern times has seen such behavior in water snakes in midsummer. The key to the problem seems to lie in the phrase "in modern times," for just over half a century ago, the great herpetologist, Raymond L. Ditmars, described a closely related species, the diamond-back water snake (*N. rhombifer*) in the Mississippi Valley where "they bask on derelict timber, or twine in clusters on stout boughs overhanging the water into which they drop upon the slightest disturbance." (*Snakes of the World*, New York: The MacMillan Co., 1931, p. 52). Perhaps, during the intervening decades too many people have persecuted these harmless snakes so that surviving *Natrix* do not form highly visible clusters like they once did.

hard put to it to keep a dutiful eye upon Homer while at the same time he bestowed a thrilling attention on the fishing pole Cedric had lent him. It was a real bamboo pole and Lorry felt proud to hold it. But there did not appear to be any fish and there was every indication that Homer would come to disaster. Despite this, however, Lorry forgot about him until electrified by a yell from his father, who had retired to a shaded spot on the bank.

Homer was sliding down one of the slippery slants of rock into water that eventually grew deep. Lorry dropped the pole and bounded to Homer's assistance. But when he landed on the shiny declivity his feet flew up and he slid on his back into the water, so that he was much in need of rescue himself. Lorry got to his feet and clasped Homer. But it was impossible to climb up the slippery slant; indeed, they slid slowly deeper and deeper, and when their father reached them with a long stick the water had come up to Homer's chin.

They were pulled out, none the worse for the experience, and the hot sun soon dried their clothes. Lorry returned to his fishing pole and Homer hunted for more holes in the rocks. Their father remained close by.[5]

Suddenly a most astonishing thing happened to Lorry. There came a sharp tug on his line. He jerked it up, over his head. Nothing else happened, except Lorry discovered the worm was gone from his hook.

"You had a bite," said his father.

"Was that—a fish?" gasped Lorry.

The smiling reply completed the realization of what was the second great fish event in Lorry's life. Never had he forgotten the first. Lorry was almost confounded. His fingers trembled so he could scarcely stick another worm on the hook. Awed, breathless, with beating heart he dropped the bait back into the green swirling water. What unknown treasure hid behind his piercing gaze. Long Lorry quivered there, waiting for a second bite. It never came.

Presently Lorry was amazed to see a strange figure of a man standing way out where the water poured over the long fall. He stood up to his bare knees in the current that foamed round his legs. He was an old man, gaunt and bowed, and he pointed a long straight fishing pole out over

---

[5]Although fifty-four conservationists and sportsmen met to form the Izaak Walton League of America at the Chicago Athletic Association in January, 1922, only one of them had the zealous determination to make this great idea something more than just an idea. Will Dilg's drive "to conserve something of the out-of-doors for the boys" was an intensely personal mission, for his only son, "his brave little fisherman" as Zane Grey once called him, had drowned some years before.

the swift water. Lorry saw that his clothes were ragged and that his gray hair protruded from a hole in his slouch hat.

"Pa, who is he?" asked Lorry.

"Well, I declare," replied his father. "That's Muddy Miser, the old fisherman."

Before he asked the question Lorry had sustained a shock of memory of his mother's warnings years ago. Fearfully he gazed now. Muddy Miser had been a terrible mystifying unreality to his childhood. But standing out there in the flesh, holding a long pole, he seemed different. Lorry forgot his own fishing to watch the old man. He stood motionless, intent on the line that slanted into the water. Lorry could have watched for hours.

"Come, boys, we must go," said his father at last; and so Lorry was rudely torn from his thrall.

The day had flown on the wings of uttermost joy. It was over, but for Lorry something indefinable and exquisite had just begun. On the start back, as he crossed the rattling-boarded covered bridge, he tarried to take a last look through the hole. How clear and swift the water ran! The roar of the falls filled his ears. He saw the solitary figure of the old fisherman standing like a statue, silhouetted against the white rapids. Lorry gazed long, wholly unconscious of the sensitiveness of his mind. Dillon's Falls was the most beautiful place in the world, a paradise of adventure; and somehow Muddy Miser was a part of it. Lorry wanted to ask his father more about the old fisherman, but something prompted him not to. Lorry had recognized Muddy Miser, yet he could not tell how. He carried away a vivid picture of the falls and the fisherman, a reality that sank deep into his unplumbed imagination.

Soon after, Lorry persuaded his mother to let him go to Joe's Run with boys of his own age and several older, upon which occasion he was initiated into the delights of bent-pin fishing. He made poor company for his companions, but by reason of his still rapture and unquenchable persistence he progressed mightily in the art of enticing and catching little silver-sided shiners. On the way home, so intent was he on preserving the minnows he carried in a tin can, that he did not join the boys in a wild chase of a chipmunk along the zigzag rail fence. For once the thrilling call:

"Ground Jimmy!" failed of attractions for Lorry. Safely home he carried his little shining fish, to place them in a tub under the hydrant, and to share the wonder of them with his brother.

The waterways through the woods took possession of Lorry, and best beloved of all was Joe's Run. Homer was denied the fun of these explorations, because in the opinion of Lorry's friends, he was not able to keep up with them. Lorry admitted it, yet that would not have made any difference to him. Homer's anguish at being left behind was not an easy thing to bear. But Lorry went and learned the inexhaustible charm of Joe's Run and its unending possibilities for new and strange fish.

This country brook meandered through open pastureland, through rustling cornfields, and between high hills heavily timbered with oak, hickory, chestnut, elm and beech.[6] The meadows blazed with the gold of dandelions and the red and white of fragrant clover. Here the water flowed murmuringly over clean pebbly bars and there ran deep and dark under a grassy bank. There were sylvan sunny glades in butternut groves, where water lost its shade of green for gold; and willow thickets where the leaves dropped in the current and catbirds called all day long.

Lorry's early career as a fisherboy had the virtue of being unspoiled by too much good luck. His beginning was ambitious, but far from spectacular. He had to labor for the little sunfish and chubs and bullheads that he caught, always spurred on and sustained by an unfaltering trust that some time he would capture a big one. Once he came near it and that was the tragic fishing catastrophe of his boyhood.

He was alone, having forged ahead of his comrades. Coming to a shady dell where the water flowed dark under a shelving rock, he dropped his bait into the gentle current and watched it sink. A flash of silver and rose deep down strung him with keen excitement. Something heavy and slow moved off with his line. If that was a bite, it was by far the mightiest he had ever experienced.

Lorry pulled up quickly. His line stopped. His reed pole bent almost double and cracked ominously, but he kept on pulling. The line described circles and cut the water with a little hiss. Then Lorry's eyes were startled by a silver and rose flash, circling, coming up, clearer, sharper. Frantically he pulled. The water splashed with a solid thump. He was lifting an enormous chub, rose and fat and speckled, beautiful as the chub of his dreams. He could scarcely lift it high enough to swing in above the rock. Then it wiggled and slipped off the pin-hook to flop back into the pool and vanish.

Lorry stared into the shadowy depths, unable to grasp the horror of his

---

[6]In an essay on "Trees" for the March 1924 issue of *Outdoor America*, Zane Grey wrote "How is an American boy, born from now on, going to be wholly American unless he can do three things—hunt for buried treasure, chase squirrels along a zigzag rail fence—and gather chestnuts in autumn? . . . There is a glory of nature passing away from the earth. My boy will never know the joys that have been mine. Something is happening to our beloved country, not the least of which is the doom of the emblem of America—forest trees."

misfortune. It could not be true. At length he realized not only the sight of this glorious chub but also that he had almost had it in his hands only to lose it. Then his heart broke. He sat there in the solitude, a victim of exceeding grief. He could only measure his yearning for that fish by the absolute new pain suffered. His sorrow was too deep for tears. There was no alleviation, no recompense, no hope. All the other fish in the world could not compare to this huge chub with his gaping mouth, his rainbow hue, his broad tail, his all that seemed the sum of the beauty and life of Joe's Run.

The August afternoon was drowsy and languorous. Only a faint breeze stirred. A snipe twittered and a crow called his melancholy notes that were supposed to presage storm. Low and far away rumbled thunder. The dreamy hum of insects filled the air, and a locust pierced the stillness with its song of waning summer. The water flowed on under Lorry, swirling and eddying to send back its soft music from the thickets and driftwood below.

As Lorry sat there alone, at last a strange thing happened to him. The solitude and loneliness, with gentle sounds in his ears, the drowsy spell of hot summer, the fragrance of the leafy dell, the movement of the water and the presence of living creatures—all these grew upon Lorry, encompassing him, forcing upon him something vague and sweet, stealing with the sensations he could not help into his mind and heart. At last out of his poignant boyish disappointment, there formed the nucleus of a growing idea—all this that he saw and felt around him, scented in the summer heat and heard on the drowsy air, was an indestructible possession, his alone, a secret recompense for any loss.

Sometimes dams were built at a bend in the stream where the water eddied and ran deep, and the gate would catch all the leaves and scum floating down, under which covering sunfish and chubs and shiners collected in hungry hordes. Here they lay in wait for the hapless insects blown by breeze into the current to drift down into the eddy. Plop! And the tiny widening circles on the water had their meaning for Lorry.

Here the great golden-bellied sunfish would bite voraciously, and the darker slimmer rock bass could be taken; and the yellow bullheads, pigs of the pool, and the bright flat-sided shiners, "high-swimmers" to the youthful angler, gave happy and exciting contrast to the sport. Many and many a lucky little fish was returned alive to the water, unhurt by the bent pin, but never until he had joined, for a time at least, his less fortunate brethren in the bucket.

There was a rare minnow for which Lorry had never learned a name. It was small, dark, with tiny golden stripes along its sides. Only once in a long while did Lorry catch one of these, and then he treasured it, and kept it long in his tub under the hydrant.[7]

September with its yellowing stream banks was a poignant reminder of the near approach of school. One more week! Another day! How the leaves fluttered in the cool wind—maple and sycamore and hickory and beech and walnut all rustling down to dot the water in varied hues! Hickory nuts and chestnuts would soon be ripe, but only for Saturdays. This was vacation time, the last day, the end of summer and of fishing.

But time and school and winter and life did not wait on Lorry's pleasure. There were hours when study and cold filled him with disgust, that only remembered joy of summer and idle days could alleviate. He had his sledding, and the snowball battles, and his skating on the shiny ponds. But in the main he did not like ice, and there were times when he hated snow. His father had a keen relish for clean fresh snow to eat, and he would send Lorry far out into the country to fetch back a pail of it untainted. To Lorry's grief his several attempts to fool his father had been detected. For when Lorry procured the snow near at hand, his father could tell by the taste that he had not gone far beyond the sooty outskirts of town to get it. And Lorry had to trudge back, and farther away.

At length the long hard hateful winter, with its lessons and restraint, passed into the cold wet spring, and the March days when the brooks were bank full of roily water, and the willows began to shine red and grow white at the tips with a fuzzy down. The sun was warm only when reflected from a bank or wall. How slowly the fields took on a tinge of green! Then the joyous Saturday when the first minnows bit sparingly in Joe's Run. The first red-breasted robin was a herald of spring. And one day the swallows came to dart and twitter and glance brightly over the waters. And so summer, with its ever-increasing joy of leafy wood and running brook, and autumn again, and then winter.

Lorry at last listened to the pleadings of Homer. He dwelt ponderingly upon the weighty problem, and in the end sacrificed the cronies of his own age for his brother. He would teach him to fish. He would make of him a companion fisherman. It was not a matter of slight moment. Even then Lorry vaguely felt it had to do with years, perhaps with all of life, certainly with something deeper than he knew.

It so happened that when the momentous day arrived late in June,

---

[7]Without more information, it is impossible to guess what "rare minnow" Lorry (alias, Pearl Gray) caught. There are several species to which this generalized description might apply, including a couple which may once have been found in the Muskingum watershed, but which are no longer there.

Lorry had fallen out of the good graces of brother Cedric and was denied the use of his fishing pole. This seemed to be a catastrophe. But as Lorry felt absolutely convinced of exceedingly unjust treatment he did not suffer many qualms at appropriating the cherished tackle without asking Cedric.

Soon Lorry and Homer were hurrying up the dusty road along the open woods toward Joe's Run, where Lorry intended to catch some minnows for bait. He had been bass fishing several times with the older boys, and though unsuccessful himself he had acquired vast stores of knowledge and ambition.

Homer proudly carried the minnow bucket and the minnow pole. He had to trot to keep up with Lorry. His rapturous excitement and amazing questions roused in Lorry a remorse that he had not taken the little brother fishing long before.

"Kin I fish, too?" was the query Homer interposed between his other questions. His freckled round face shone with the brightness of adventure. He had forgotten to wear a cap and his red hair blazed in the sun.

They arrived at Joe's Run and, like Indians, stealthily stalked along the bank, talking in whispers. Arriving at a favorite hole under the big elm tree, Lorry proceeded to put a piece of worm on his hook and drop it into the water. Soon he jerked out a nice chub, and another and another until he had ten or a dozen good live baits in the bucket. With that he let Homer use the minnow pole, and sat close by with great store of advice. Homer jerked his first chub back over his head, at the same moment emitting a squeal of joy. On succeeding bites Lorry had trouble keeping Homer from repeating these performances. But at last the lad achieved something that augured well for the future. Whereupon they took up the bucket, waded the run, crossed the road and entered the cornfield, where the green waving blades of cornstalks were already higher than Homer's head.

In due time they got into pasture land and again came to Joe's Run. Here it was deep and still, and flowed between high slanting banks. Lorry pointed out a place for Homer. "There's a good hole," he said. "If we need more bait we'll try it."

On the far side of the meadow ran Licking Creek, a beautiful stream, shaded by elms and sycamores. Along its banks there were open benches and rock ledges, and other attractive places to fish from. Lorry tried a live minnow in each attractive spot without success. But he kept on going upstream as tense and hopeful as at the first. Homer's more youthful anticipation suffered a blight. "You ain't agoin' to ketch any bass," he averred.

"Homer, that's no way to talk," responded Lorry. "You gotta keep on thinkin' you're goin' to ketch some."

Presently they came to a high brushy bank from which Lorry espied a fallen sycamore that extended out into the stream. To get down and out on this log was going to be a hard task for them, but Lorry felt that once there, something wonderful would happen. He got down himself, and had Homer hand down the bucket and pole. Lorry placed these carefully in a safe place on the log, then attended to the more difficult task of helping Homer down. From earliest childhood, Homer had never evinced any skill in climbing down a place or up one, either. He was chubby and rather awkward. Twice he slipped on the steep bank and but for Lorry's frantic clutch would have gone into the water, which was deep between the log and the bank.

This fallen tree had gnarled branches, broken and bleached, that made it a safe place to stand or walk. The water on the outside was deep and dark, with alluring lights under the side of the trunk that stretched out into the stream. There was a swift current gliding along.

"You set there an' watch," said Lorry to his brother, pointing to a comfortable fork in a branch.

"Kin I fish some here?" queried Homer.

Lorry put a cork on his line about three feet above the sinker, and then kneeling over the bucket he caught a chub in his left hand, and gently hooked it through the lips. This done he stood up and cast the bait out into the current and let it float down into an eddy caused by driftwood that had lodged against the log.

"Keep your eye on the cork," admonished Lorry.

Homer's gaze was riveted on that floating cork and his expression was one of utter wild expectation.

Lorry, however, though he always had that cork in the tail of his eye, had sight for many other things. The day was in June, rich in the fresh green of early summer. A kingfisher fluttered above the creek, moving from one aerial station to another, as he watched for his prey, and presently shot down like a plummet. A killdeer ran along the sandy margin of the bank, under the blossoming vines. Orioles and blackbirds made contrasting and exquisite melody in the sycamores. Meadow larks flew across the creek, uttering their piercing sweet notes. The sky was azure, with a few fleecy clouds. The fresh dank smells of spring and high water still lingered in the air.

"Lorry, your cork's under!" suddenly shrieked Homer.

"I saw it go," whispered Lorry tensely. "Set still. It's a bass!"

The shadow of the sinking cork faded in the depths. Lorry quivered all over. He must wait a second longer, but he could not. Mightily he jerked. He came up hard on a solid live weight that pulled the pole down. The line described a circle, in the midst of which came a great splash. Lorry saw what seemed an enormous bronze-backed fish, mouth wide open, fin erect, tail curled—a bass.

The following moments were as one terrible age of confusion and stress. What happened Lorry did not clearly see and could not truly guess. But the period ended with Lorry finding himself straddling the log. He had hold of the bass through mouth and gills. The minnow bucket had been overturned and lay precariously. Lorry's heart left his throat. He put the rod down and took a string from his pocket. This he slipped through the gills of the fish and tied the other end to a snub of branch. Whereupon he lifted the bass out for Homer's edification.

"Look!" he cried.

Homer was incapable of voicing the awe and rapture his staring eyes expressed. The bass might have weighed a pound. But he was Lorry's first bass, beautifully bronzed and marked, with angrily spread dorsal, and eyes gleaming darkly red. Lorry let him down into the water on the inside of the log. Then he espied the minnow bucket he had overturned.

With a start he grasped it. There was a little water left, and one minnow.

"All gone 'cept a chub," he sighed tragically.

"Aw!" cried Homer.

Lorry pondered a moment. Sight of the captured bass curling his fins brought some consolation to that awful moment. Then he put the last bait on his hook and dropped it into the water.

"Homer, I'll tell you what," he said suddenly. "You ketch some minnows."

"Me!" I'll go—you bet," replied Homer, with vast assurance.

Lorry threw the bucket up on the bank, and the can of worms after it. Then by dint of extreme effort he boosted Homer far enough to catch the vines.

"The minnow pole is up there," said Lorry. "Go to the deep place I showed you—the last one. Catch some an' hurry back."

Homer vanished through the green foliage. Whereupon Lorry took up the pole and once more attended to the fascinating watch of that cork. Gradually his excitement subsided. It seemed he was not going to have another bite right off. Something cast a blight upon the marvel of the hour. It oppressed Lorry. At length he discovered the reason—he should not have sent Homer off alone.

Lorry was in a quandary. Here was the wonderful day—precious moments on the creek—and he could not stay. He must not stay longer. Homer was only a little tad. He might fall in the creek or get lost. Lorry reproached himself, and manfully fought the almost irresistible temptation to go on fishing. But then for the first time he realized he cared more for Homer than anyone, except their mother, and he could not stay.

Taking pole and bass he climbed the bank, and set into a run along the shady winding path of bare packed sand. It seemed a long while before he reached the mouth of Joe's Run. Here he slowed to a walk and followed the edge of the bank.

It was now only a short distance to the deep place where he had directed Homer to go. Lorry reached it. No sign of Homer! Filled with dismay and growing concern Lorry again broke into a run. What would mother say—if anything happened? But Lorry knew he would never go home without his brother. Suddenly he heard a cry. It came from beyond a patch of willows.

"I'm—comin'!" he called.

He bounded along beyond the willows to a high bank. Like the one below, it slanted to the water. In the middle of it lay Homer, head down, on his stomach. His arms were outstretched and he appeared to be slowly sliding down. His bare toes were digging into the dirt.

"Homer! For the land's sake!" yelled Lorry. "What're you doin' there?"

"Fish!—Whad-dye spose—you dum fool—hurry!" panted Homer.

Then Lorry made the astounding discovery that Homer was holding to the butt end of the minnow pole, which was half submerged. Something was tugging hard on it. Lorry saw a swirl in the water.

"Hang on!" he yelled, and plunged down, just in the nick of time to save Homer from sliding in. Lorry grasped his brother and hauled him back. "Hang to the pole!"

"I'm—ahangin'!" said Homer valiantly.

Lorry got him turned round with his feet on a level place. But the fish, whatever it was, appeared too heavy and strong for Homer.

"Gimme the pole!" cried Lorry, almost roughly.

"Aw, he's my—fish," gasped Homer, clinging for dear life to the pole.

"All right, hang on, an' I'll help," said Lorry, and suiting action to words he laid hands over Homer's. But this was not to pull hard, for Lorry distrusted the line and hook. It had happened, however, that on the way from Joe's Run to Licking Creek he had put a larger hook on the line, intending to let Homer use it for sunfish. This he had forgotten.

The remembrance encouraged Lorry in the hope they could catch the fish. So he merely helped Homer hold the pole while the fish swam round until it got tired.

Lorry saw a bright red tail and then he knew what kind of fish they had. Presently he got the line in his hand, and slipping the fish out of the mud he grasped it and carried it in triumph up the bank. Homer had hung to him like a leech.

"There!" exclaimed Lorry, dropping the prize on the grass. "Big red-horse sucker!"

Homer dropped on his knees in an ecstasy and he babbled in glee. The fish was a foot and a half long, glistening white all over, except the tip of his tail, which was red.

"Ooo-oooo!" crooned Homer.

"Say, Bub," queried Lorry, severely, suddenly remembering something. "Why didn't you let go that pole?"

"Lorry—I couldn't," replied Homer.

"Why not, I'd like to know?" demanded Lorry. "He was pullin' you in."

"I didn't care. . . . I couldn't let go—an' I wouldn't if I could!"

The answer silenced Lorry, and in the after years he recalled it many times. Moreover, to add mightily to Homer's performance, he had caught two small rock bass, which were alive in the bucket.

Flushed with victory the boys hurried home, and arrived before supper time. Their father, as was his custom on a summer evening, sat in his chair on the lawn. Homer ran across the grass, dragging his trophy, the red-horse sucker, to burst into breathless acclaim.

"What the Sam Hill!" ejaculated the father, staring from the fish to Homer. "Did you catch this fish?"

"Yes, pa," began the lad.

While he was reciting in wild and whirling words the story of his capture Lorry stood by, reluctant to exhibit his black bass, because it might detract from Homer's triumph. Their mother came to the door.

"Go wash your dirty hands and feet," she said, trying to look severe.

As they fled round the corner of the house Lorry heard his mother say: "Did you ever see two happier boys? They just love to fish."

At the hydrant the boys deposited their fish, and put the live rock bass into the tub. Then, as Lorry bent over to wash, he received a kick by no means mild. He leaped erect, furious, knowing full well whence that kick came. Cedric stood there, glaring down on him.

"Stole my fish pole again, didn't you?" he demanded, threateningly.

"Yes, I did—but don't you ever dare kick me again," answered Lorry, stoutly.

Cedric resembled all elder brothers in that he could not see a halo round the head of any boy. He aimed another kick at Lorry that fell just short. Lorry was as nimble as a goat. He ran, and Cedric ran after him. They had this race often. But on the last occasion Lorry had hidden his baseball bat behind an evergreen. As he rounded the bushy tree he snatched out the bat and had it swinging when Cedric charged right upon him.

"Hyar—you little devil!" yelled Cedric, suddenly halting, and frantically bending to avoid the bat. But Lorry was too quick. The bat thudded hard on Cedric's hip. He staggered and sagged.

"You will—keep on—kickin' me!" shouted Lorry, bravely, though the second the blow fell he was ready to drop with fear. But Cedric, without a word, limped away toward the house. And he never kicked Lorry again.

Homer babbled in his slumber that night, to the extent of keeping Lorry awake, and even waking his mother in the next room. She called out: "Lorry, shake your brother. He is having a nightmare."

"No, mar, he's only hangin' on to a fish," replied Lorry, giggling. Nevertheless he gave Homer a shake.

"Aw—he's my fish," wailed Homer, in the midst of this rude rousing.

Much to Lorry's gratification, the red-horse sucker had made Homer a fisherboy all in one day. Before, Homer had merely yearned to go along with his brother and the older boys; now he had won fame and was finding it sweet. Also it was hard to sustain. Homer enticed youngsters of his own age to run off to Joe's Run, whereby he received punishment, and earned another kind of reputation in the neighborhood.

Now and then Lorry took Homer with him on excursions to Joe's Run, or Timber Run, which was a rival of the smaller brook. Bartlett's Run and Flesher's Run were farther afield than Lorry had yet roamed. What he had heard of them, however, was enticing. And Poverty Run— farther still—had a glamor about its vague legends of wonderful minnows. The older boys said that Poverty Run emptied into Licking Creek five miles above Dillon's Falls and was a paradise for bass. Somewhere along its mouth was a secret rock ledge known only to Old Muddy Miser.

In addition to taking Homer with him occasionally, Lorry told the lad all that he heard about the different runs, about fish and fishing. But Homer seemed to be a true son of Izaak Walton in that the only peace and contentment for him was in actually fishing himself.

One summer evening Homer had not come home by supper time. His mother was worried. She accused Lorry, who disclaimed any knowledge of Homer's whereabouts.

"Find him before your father comes home," she said. "Maybe he's playing on Madden's Hill."

Lorry ran over to the hill, and through the woods, and across the commons. No sign of Homer! None of the other boys had seen him. The matter began to look serious to Lorry. He hurried over to Tom Linden's, a particular playmate of Homer's.

"Naw, I don't know nuthin' about where Homer went," said Tom, in apparent disgust. "I know he was goin' fishin' with some boys, an' I couldn't go because I had to mow the lawn."

Further inquiry led to some rather vague information about Homer in company with a new set of boys going to Sunderland's Lake.

Lorry hurried back home, to see his father entering the yard. At this moment the tall spare figure, with its long black coat and high plug hat, was hardly a welcome one. Lorry had incurred his father's displeasure by fostering a desire for fishing in Homer's breast. But Lorry bravely faced both father and mother, and on the moment lost his dread. Her sweet sad anxious face somehow lent him strength.

"No, I didn't find Homer, but I will," he replied to her anxious query. "Don't worry, mother."

"You better had, and quick, too, you young Muddy Miser," declared his father. "I'll go out and cut me a nice apple switch."

The threat of a switching had no particular effect on Lorry. He would have been glad to take a dozen switchings, if they would only fetch Homer back. Lorry ran across the lawn, through Wedge's orchard and Lee's pasture to the road. His feet were bare and the dust felt soft and cool. He ran clear out into the country before he slowed down to catch his breath. Sunderland's Lake was his only clue. Sunderland was a farmer in ill repute with the boys. He had a beautiful little dark deep lake set down between two grassy hills. It was full of big golden sunfish. And Sunderland would not allow the boys to fish in it. Not even when he was begged! This put him out of the pale of all youngsters and prompted the bolder of them to watch when he drove to town, and then steal an hour's fishing in the enchanted lake.

Lorry clung to his hope that Homer had gone there with some older lads. The distance was quite five miles, which would account for the late hour. But he knew Homer might as well have gone to the mouth of Joe's Run, another forbidden swimming hole made dreadful by two drownings.

Only last summer Clarence Linden had been drowned there. The remembrance stopped Lorry's heart. He had seen Clarence when they brought him home—purple-faced, all wet and limp, so strange and cold. He remembered Mrs. Linden and Tom, and the sisters—how terrible they had carried on. Suppose Homer had— ! But Lorry fought the thought that he had seen in his mother's eyes. He broke into a run again, stern and hard in his determination to find Homer.

Meanwhile darkness was coming on. The drowsy summer night was at hand. Lorry heard the chirp of crickets, the bleat of sheep, the call of a whippoorwill. This last always made his flesh creep, so weird and strange did it seem, so wild and lonely. Even when snug and safe in bed to hear a whippoorwill would make him shiver.

At length he came to the forks of the road, one of which led to Frazeysburg and the other to Dresden. Here must be his last decision. One road led round to Joe's Run, and the other straight out by Sunderland's Lake. Lorry chose the latter. By and by he got out of breath again and had to slow to a walk.

The dusk seemed full of shadows and forms. Lorry had always feared the dark. As a child it had been peopled with ghosts, fairies, giants, monsters, ogres; and as a youth he still saw the same unrealities and believed in them. This time he was not afraid. But the pang of dread for Homer spread through his breast; and when pitch darkness settled down Lorry was close to panic.

All at once he heard a cry, far ahead in the dark. It halted him. How he trembled as he listened! His mouth was dry and his body cold. The cry came again, fainter, and it struck Lorry's heart. Swift as a deer he ran on up the dark dusty road, calling aloud.

Soon through the gloom he espied a dim little figure—a boy, in white cotton blouse and short pants—bareheaded and barelegged. It was his brother. Going the wrong way!

"Oh, Homer, I've—found you!" panted Lorry. He did not need to be told that Homer was lost and terribly frightened. The lad clutched him wildly and sobbed out incoherently. For Lorry the moment was tremendous. Homer was safe. He had found him. He must hurry home so as to reassure his mother. He took his brother's hand and set off down the dark road, walking so fast that Homer had to trot to keep up.

After a while Homer ceased crying.

"Where are the other boys?" asked Lorry.

"They got on a wagon before dark," said Homer. "I couldn't ketch it."

"You should not go with boys who run off from you."

"I won't—never again," replied Homer.

"How'd you get lost!" asked Lorry.

"We was in a field—when the old farmer chased us," said Homer, breathlessly. "We come to a fence an' a cross-road. A wagon drove along. I couldn't ketch it. . . . . I run an' run. The wagon went out of sight. It got all dark. The road went into another road. An' I didn't know which way to go."

Lorry took advantage of the occasion to impress upon Homer's mind the need of always watching where he went, looking at fences, trees, farmhouses, hills, and roads so he would remember them.

"Oh, Lorry—I was so glad—you came. I was scared turrible—First when I found I was lost—I thought you'd come—then when you didn't I thought you never would.

"Is pa very mad?" asked Homer, as if suddenly confronted with an entirely new and direful phase of the situation.

"Yes, an' he's goin' to whip us both with an apple switch."

"You! What fer? You didn't do nuthin'," declared Homer.

"Pa thinks it's my fault you ran off fishin'—an' I guess it is."

"Lorry, I won't run off again. I won't have you gettin' whipped fer me."

"I don't mind whippin's or how mad pa gets. It's mother I feel bad about."

"Oh, is she mad, too?" asked Homer, in changed voice.

"No. She was just scared. I know she was thinkin' you'd gone to the mouth of Joe's Run, where Tom's brother drowned."

Homer was silent for a long time. Lorry heard the catch in his breath and felt a closer clasp of the little hand on his. They tramped on homeward over the dusty country road in the thick starless night.

"Lorry, you'll have to take me fishin' more," said Homer, solemnly, as if propounding a grave and momentous conclusion.

"Looks like it," replied Lorry, in as serious a tone.

CHAPTER II

Lorry had not made a mistake about the dire possibilities of his father's reaction to Homer's latest fishing adventure. Not that night, however, but the morning after, both boys were taken separately into the large unfurnished parlor of the house, where they made further acquaintance with the apple switch.

This punishment did not result in any improvement in the behavior of the brothers, according to Mrs. Dunn's confidence to a neighbor, but it

did keep in Lorry's memory the need to look after Homer. That boy bade fair to grow up bad, and what was worse, to be a poor fisherman. So for several years, during spring and summer, Lorry faithfully trained the little fellow in the arts of minnow angling. Dillon's Falls remained a haunting memory until Homer was eleven years old. He had grown out of his pudginess into a tall strong lad with red hair and freckled face. Lorry at fourteen was not large, but remarkably athletic and fleet of foot. Next to fishing, baseball was their favorite pastime. In the fall, rabbit and squirrel hunting took them often into the fields and woods but seldom had they the opportunity to accompany anyone with guns. Their weapons were primitive sling-shots with which Lorry grew to be so deadly that he could hit a bird on the wing.

On several never-to-be-forgotten occasions, their father took them hunting; and thus a rival of the fishing instinct developed in them. It did not, however, ever gain the ascendancy, even in those wild days of boyhood when the killing instinct stirs most powerfully. Hunting was a game for frosty autumn woods, and for the snow-covered hills.

Homer grew to be a stripling youth quite capable of taking care of himself among boys of his own age. He and Tom Linden and a boon companion they called Smitty formed a triangle quite as inseparable, if not so adventurous, as any of those of Lorry's earlier years. Tom Linden never learned to fish, but he never ceased trying; Smitty was an eager and apt pupil of Homer's. And Joe's Run from the slaughter house to the falls came to know the imprint of their bare feet.

Naturally these new friendships of Homer's had their effect on Lorry. Secretly he was jealous and resented them, yet he felt something of shame, and a gladness that his brother was growing up. Lorry did not confess to himself that one of the reasons he welcomed Homer's independence was because of a disturbing new element which had slipped into his life. Girls!

Both Homer and Tom were mild-tempered boys, which was unlike the dispositions of some of their companions. Perhaps the two boys also had sharp tongues, which might have accounted for the fights they got into. Not a week passed that Lorry did not rescue them from the Eighth Ward boys. Once Homer came in with a black eye, for which he would give little account. All that Lorry could find out was there had been a quarrel over a fishing pole. Homer certainly did not have the pole, and just as surely he did have a black eye.

One Saturday in the spring of this important year Lorry returned from town, where he had been bound to the hateful work in his father's office, to find a baseball game in progress on Madden's Hill. He heard the yelling of the boys, and as it did not sound like the usual joy and fun of a ball game, he leaped the fence and hurried out to the hill.

Madden's Hill was a favorite playground of the boys of the Terrace. It was a wide green common, verging on the edge of a steep sandbank, that slanted down to the road below. Here Lorry had many a time hidden on the brink to throw eggs and walnuts at Old Daddy Howe or Andy Sunderland as they drove by.

Lorry reached the hill to find the ball game broken up into a fight. The boys were grouped in a moving circle from which emanated yells and cries. As Lorry drew near, he was both amazed and infuriated to see Homer break out of the crowd, blood streaming from his nose, and run with a fleetness for which he was noted. Harry Tomans, brandishing a ball bat and yelling at the top of his lungs, was pursuing him. Lorry thought that he had arrived in the nick of time. Looking about for a weapon he espied a piece of brick which he grasped and with a loud, "Drop that bat!" he raced to meet Harry.

This turned the chase the other way, but Harry did not drop the bat. He ran toward the crowd on the edge of the sandbank, yelling back, "I'll knock your head off."

Lorry, halting short, threw the brick. It hit Harry on the back and knocked him flat. The ball bat went flying down the sandbank. But Harry was little hurt, he leaped up, bawling with rage and stood his ground. The fact that his brother Jake came running out of the crowd lent him courage. Lorry found himself confronted by the two brothers on the brink of the sandbank.

Lorry rushed them, and with a quick blow sent Harry over the edge. Then he and Jake fought to and fro along the edge to the delight of the following, howling mob. When Harry, breathless and covered with sand, clambered over the edge of the bank, Lorry knocked Jake off. He rolled clear to the bottom. Harry, nothing daunted, plunged to strike wildly at Lorry. Maneuvering around, Lorry presently delivered a hard blow to Harry's nose. Harry fell on the edge of the bank. It gave way under him and he slid down to the wild yells of the boys.

"Better—stay down!" panted Lorry.

Jake yelled up his defiance and fury and the terrible things he would do. When Harry joined him the two of them crawled to the rim and tried to climb over. But Lorry beat them off and again sent Jake rolling. Whereupon Harry reached for stones, which he flung at Lorry. This act did not find favor with the watching boys. They jeered at him. Then Jake, as game as he was mad, climbed like a monkey back to the rim. This time he tried to get up at a place some yards from Harry, and had almost succeeded when Lorry pushed him down. Meanwhile Harry got his knees up on a level, and was clinging desperately when Lorry got back to him. This time Lorry let him rise to his feet before he hit him. Harry screamed and fell off the rim and bounded down in a most alarming manner. Then Lorry ran back to Jake, who had got a good hold of the level ground.

"I—can lick—you," panted Jake, "but I—gotta nough for—today."

Lorry helped Jake up to the level. Harry did not appear to be badly hurt. He crawled out of the sand and got to his feet and gazed upward with a dirty and bloody face. He shook a menacing fist, but he was voiceless.

"How'd he come to be chasin' you with that bat?" demanded Lorry later of the pale faced Homer.

"Aw, he took my place," replied Homer, "an' he hit me in the nose. I grabbed up the bat. He pulled out his knife. I swung on him—knocked the knife out of his hand. Then we fought for the bat . . . He's bigger'n me. He got it. Then I ran."

"You keep out of Harry's road," replied Lorry soberly.

Longed-for vacation came at last, and that was a glorious event, which for the time being made all school boys friends.

The summer before this one Lorry had become acquainted with three boys, brothers, who lived beyond the Terrace in a region known as Bald Hill. Their names were Ed, Luce, and Crow Graves. Their father was dead, and their uncles were market-fishermen, hard-drinking, hard-working men upon whom, of course, the Terrace people looked down. Crow was the eldest, a powerful youth of sixteen, coarse-featured and crude, not given much to school or work. He had both fishing instincts and skill, and was one boy Lorry particularly liked to fish with. Ed was an undersized boy, shifty of eye, vicious of disposition; and he was not friendly toward Lorry. Luce, the youngest, was a tall lanky lad, lean-faced and tow-headed, an ardent lover of fishing, and governed wholly by whom he happened to be with at the moment.

With these three boys Lorry planned to go to Dillon's Falls, a long anticipated jaunt. Early morning of the first day of vacation found them padding the cool dust of the road, loaded with buckets of bait and a basket of food, and their poles.

Lorry exhibited his fishing pole with a strange shy pride. It was a long bamboo, straight as an arrow. He had wound black thread around it to hold the wire guides and the tip, for the line to run freely from the reel. The reel was nickel-plated, of fair size, and held a brand new white linen line. The boys gazed and handled this outfit with admiring envy. Lorry did not acquaint them with the circumstances leading to the possession of such fine tackle. No boy in Hainesville had ever owned one equal to it. Lorry had worked to earn the money to purchase it. Twice a week for months he had gone to town before breakfast to sweep out his father's office, and every day for the same period he had saved the ten cents allowed him for lunch. He had gone without anything to eat at the noon hour during those school days.

Spring had been late yielding to summer. Here it was almost the third week in June, and the maple leaves were just full-foliaged, and the creamy candelabra-like blossoms of the chestnuts shone in the thick, rich, amber light. The golden orioles were nesting in the walnut trees, and flickers and red-headed woodpeckers hammered on dead trees. Over all had settled the sweet, wonderful drowsy glamour of early summer.

The boys walked fast, with tongues as lively as their feet. A large anticipation, the inborn thing so characteristic of fishermen, prompted their conjectures and boasts. The kingdom of adventure was in their hearts. They walked the distance from Brush's woods to the Falls in an hour. Lorry thrilled while crossing the loose-boarded floor of the covered bridge. He could see the swift green water through the cracks. His eye, already wonderfully keen, sighted the shadowy forms of the fish in the shallow water. How endless had been the days, months, years that had elapsed since his first visit to this enchanting place! Yet though ages had seemed to pass, it was exactly as he remembered it. Only greener, brighter, more beautiful! Lorry wondered if he would again see the old hermit fisherman who haunted this stretch of waterfall.

The boys almost ran through the grove of sycamores and thorn trees down to Big Rock. What was their amazed and sickening disappointment to find the coveted fishing place already occupied by other boys. Tway Miller, Keith Horn, Frank Pierce, Harry Tomans, and several more not well known to Lorry, gazed up at the late comers with all the disdain of conscious superiority.

"Ketch any?" asked Crow Graves.

"Naw!" replied Keith.

"T-t-t-tw-tw-two b-b-bi-bites," stuttered Tway Miller.

"Fishin' fer bass or suckers?" went on Crow, with his sharp eye roving.

"Fishing for whatever'll bite," said Frank Pierce with sarcasm.

"You wouldn't know what was bitin' if you did get a bite," averred Crow in like spirit.

It was plain that the anglers who had gotten there first did not like this encroachment upon their preserve. These boys all went to the same school, and played baseball together, but this fishing was a different matter.

Lorry knew nothing of the ethics of anglers. Under no circumstances, however, would he have cast a line near those other boys. He picked out a place quite apart, so poor a place in their estimation that they jeered at him.

"Haw! Haw! you an' your new fishin' pole!" taunted Harry Tomans.

Lorry noted that Harry sat high up on the rock with a rifle beside him. He was the one boy who did not fish. Lorry soon forgot him and for that matter, his own companions. As luck would have it, he almost at once got a bite. The fish stripped the hook of worms. Next time the tense and alert Lorry was ready for that delicate nibble, and he hooked the fish. It gave a good stiff fight and turned out to be a red-horse sucker nearly two feet long. The boys saw Lorry land it and yelled their satisfaction or envy, according to their dispositions. Crow Graves and Luce took up positions close to Lorry. Soon Lorry caught another red-horse almost as large as the first. That settled any indecision. All the youthful fishermen except Harry Tomans, surrounded Lorry.

"What you baitin' with?" asked one.

"T-t-t-te-tell m-m-m-mme how you f-f-f-fish," begged the stuttering Tway.

"How deep's your lead?"

"Did you spit on your bait?"

Lorry preserved a serenity that was far more a result of his success than his natural disposition to be unruffled under such circumstances. He knew in his heart it was just luck. But he spoke with a profound and mysterious wisdom of a science of angling far beyond their ken. He might as well have claimed to have a knowledge of fish language.

For a long time the simple ardent boys accorded him this supremacy.

However, good luck did not again visit Lorry. The hours sped by. The boys tired and changed from place to place. Some of them waded out along the rocky shelves and reefs of the falls. But as the water was still high, they did not go far nor have any success. Toward afternoon the air grew warm, almost hot. Again both groups of boys congregated upon Big Rock; and as they had apparently exhausted the possibilities of fishing they went in swimming.

Lorry did not stay in long. The water was cold and he hated it as he hated winter, ice and gray bleak days. When he had put on his clothes he sat on the side of the shelving rock and watched the boys. Crow Graves was an expert diver and swimmer. It was a splendid sight to see him dive from a height. They played bannerman, which was a game where the leader executed daring feats for the others to follow. When they tired of this they resorted to a sport common to boys—that of mud slinging.

Lorry had tied his two fish to a willow, several rods up the sandy bank from the rock. He found them still alive, and as was his wont he watched them, admiring their beauty, knowing well he should mercifully kill them, yet loth to do so.

As he climbed back to the shelving rock, which at that point stood a few feet above the willows, he espied Old Muddy Miser wading along the shore with a long fishing pole extended over the water. He carried a battered bucket, evidently made from a powder can. Lorry was so surprised and thrilled that he uttered a little cry. The old fisherman looked precisely the same as when Lorry had first seen him. He was tall and gaunt. A black slouch hat hid part of his worn gray face. Straggling gray locks of hair protruded from the holes in his hat. His coat was very ragged. His trousers, of like appearance, were rolled above his knees, exposing lean brown legs. He was fishing down along the bank, and when now and then he made a slow, easy cast, Lorry saw that his bait was a live minnow. For a moment the old childish fear of this man returned to Lorry. Then he dismissed it and wished the other boys were not there. What would they do or say when the old man came in sight?

CHAPTER III

Lorry did not have to wait long to find out. Harry Tomans was the first to espy the fisherman.

"Hey, boys, here comes Old Muddy Miser," he called from his vantage point. "Let's have some fun."

The naked boys climbed to him, eager, mischievous, easy prey to suggestion. Lorry did not like the looks of things. He went towards them, and ascended the slanting part of Big Rock, until he stood on top, above them. He had no idea what they would do, or how he would act.

Old Muddy Miser waded along the shore until he reached the edge of the shelving ledge and here he left the water to fish from the rock. If he saw or heard the boys he made no sign. Gradually he walked along the ledge. Lorry was keen to note how he manipulated that live bait. Suddenly a stone swooped over the fisherman's head and dropped with a splash near his line. Lorry whirled quickly. He saw that Harry Tomans had thrown that stone. The boys were snickering and had their backs turned when the old man lifted his gray face to look at them. How strangely that old face affected Lorry! Soon it was averted, and the fisherman gave no further heed. Some of the other boys threw gravel into the water where he was fishing.

"That's a dirty trick," called Lorry, sharply. "Would you want anybody to throw stones in where you were fishing?"

"Pogie! Pogie! Pogie!" yelled Harry Tomans with his back turned.

This ill-sounding epithet was one given to inmates of the County Poor House. Old Muddy Miser had no home, and in the winter he lived on the charity of the county. This fact was known to all. Lorry gasped with an emotion new to him. He suffered a shock that any boy could so revile an old man, especially an old inoffensive fisherman.

Ed Graves reached for a rock that lay at his feet.

"Don't you throw it," called Lorry, low and hard.

Ed seemed checked in his movement. He gazed up at Lorry, his shrifty eyes expressing anger and doubt. The chances seemed that he would risk Lorry's disfavor and throw the rock. But his brother Crow pushed him back.

"Say, don't you like to fish?" he said, gruffly.

Then Harry Tomans snatched up a stone and cast it, not carelessly or mischievously, but with the malice that was in him. The stone nearly hit the old man.

"I'll fix you for that, Harry Tomans," shouted Lorry fiercely.

"Bah, what can you do?" yelled back Harry.

With the flame of fury which suddenly burned over him, Lorry saw the hour he had long expected had come. Swiftly grasping a lump of sun-baked mud, the only missile within reach, he threw it hard at Harry. The lump cracked on his bare back and burst into dust. Harry screamed as if stung by a whip. Bawling incoherently he ran to where his rifle lay on his clothes, and cocking it he pointed it up at Lorry.

"Damn you! I'll kill you!" Harry shouted.

Lorry gazed down into the evil face, and into the tiny round black hole in the end of the rifle. A terrible calm waved over him. Deliberately he knelt, bent his head and began to tie the lace of his canvas shoe. His fingers trembled slightly. Lorry heard some of the boys gasp, as if the suspense had suddenly broken. Then Harry growled; "You look out for me, Lorry Dunn!"

Lorry felt released from a mighty strain. He raised his head. Harry had lowered the rifle and was in the act of stepping aside. Manifestly he had taken Lorry's strange action to mean he had been intimidated. Letting down the hammer of the rifle Harry walked over to his clothes and laid it down.

The tension among the boys relaxed. Tway Miller began to stutter: "L-l-l-le-let's go home."

But every nerve in Lorry's body was strung for action. When Harry swaggered back to the circle of his comrades Lorry leaped like a tiger off the rock and pounced upon the rifle. He flung it far out into the river. With that same wild action he bounded upon Harry, beat him down and knocked him off the rock into the river. He went under, came up sputtering water and blood, and floundered to the ledge. He climbed out, bawling with insane rage. The instant he got up on the level bench he began to search for some kind of weapon. He threw a bucket and a shoe at Lorry's head. Lorry dodged them and then rushed in to batter him with lightning blows. Harry was heavy, clumsy. He swung at random. Lorry knocked him flat. Harry got to his knees and began to crawl round looking for things to throw. He found a piece of sharp rock, and flung it with all his might, edgewise, and the missile just grazed Lorry's head as he ducked. Lorry welcomed this boy's code of fighting. He jumped with both feet square upon Harry, bowling him over on the ledge. Harry struggled to rise, and Lorry, with all his might, kicked him in the face, knocking him into the water. Harry went under. He did not come up quickly.

The older Graves boy dove in and came up, dragging Harry with him.

"Help, you—fellers!" yelled Crow.

Several of them went to his assistance, and soon they dragged Harry to safety on the rock. Blood ran in a red stream from his nose and mouth, down over his chin and to his wet body. He was conscious, but at last thoroughly beaten. While Lorry watched, breathing heavily, the boys wiped the blood off Harry and helped him on with his shirt.

Lorry walked out of hearing and sat down. He suddenly found himself so weak he could not stand, aware of a quivering and jerking of his muscles, of the sweat that made him wringing wet, of the laboring breast. The terrible commotion within him was a fearful thing. A dark tide of his mind seemed to be wavering, receding. For some moments he sat there, with head bent, sick and spent. Then as he gradually recovered something of his composure, he felt extreme pain in his right foot. This was the one with which he had kicked Harry so violently. His knuckles were skinned and there was a bad bruise on his left knee.

Both groups of boys gathered up their poles and buckets, and climbed the rock.

"We're goin' home," called Crow Graves, walking a few paces along the ledge. He seemed uncertain, yet was plainly friendly.

"Leave me alone," answered Lorry.

Crow hesitated a moment, then joining the others, disappeared with them under the green sycamores. Lorry heard the clink of a tin bucket on stone. Turning, he saw the old fisherman standing just below on the sand. His face and shoulders came abreast of the ledge where Lorry sat. That old face was seamed and worn, with scant gray beard, and hooked nose, and weary, sad eyes, gray as his hair. They bore a gaze of inquiry.

"Lad, what is your name?"

"Lorry Dunn."

"Is your father Dr. Dunn?"

"Yes, sir."

"I knew him years ago." Then the old man opened his bucket and took out the only fish it contained—a bass larger than Lorry had ever seen before. "Here, you take this."

"Thank you," exclaimed Lorry. "What a whopper!"

"Do you like to fish?"

"Yes, sir—love it," answered Lorry, with a shy eagerness.

"Come and fish with me some day," said Old Muddy Miser. "I live in the pot-shop at the head of the falls."

"Oh—I will," stammered Lorry.

Then the old man picked up his bucket and shouldering his long pole he started into the willows. As Lorry stared at the bent form, the old slouch hat, the old man turned to say, "I'm glad you are not like those other boys."

Lorry knew something wonderful and profound had happened.

He sat for a long time, dreaming, listening to the murmur of the running water, wondering about this strange old fisherman until the cool shade of the trees warned him that the sun was setting.

He put the bass on the string with his red-horse suckers and taking up his rod he started home. His foot hurt considerably, but he could walk, and did not mind the pain. As he crossed the covered bridge he peeped through one of the cracks in the wall to look long at the white and green stretch of water. Dillon's Falls! Something significant had come into his life—the beginning of a fulfillment of vague romance, of the kingdom of adventure.

"Yes, I'll come," he said softly to himself, and then walked on, rattling the loose boards of the floor of the bridge.

Lorry reached home just before dark. As usual his father sat out on the lawn in his easy chair.

"For the land's sake!" he ejaculated, in great pleasure. "Lorry, you are a—a—lucky boy."

Lorry well knew that his father had intended to say fisherman, and he swelled with pride. His mother beamed on him with her soft dark eyes. Homer came rushing up and babbled praise incoherently.

The story of Lorry's fight with Harry Tomans did not pass beyond the several circles of boys living in the Eighth Ward and on the Terrace; and Lorry's dread that his father would learn of it and forbid his going to Dillon's Falls gradually wore away.

After that adventure Lorry found the early days of his long vacation beset with contending tides of longing. He scarcely realized why picnics and parties had suddenly acquired an unaccountable fascination. It was not the rides and the games and the merry picnic dinners spread in the green grass under the shady elms and maples. There was something stronger than these, and at last he reduced it to a strange mixture of color and movement and life—the blue and white frocks, the trim ankles and dancing feet, the sunlit charm of glossy brown and golden braids, the sweetness of eyes—black, gray, violet—all that was wonderful and mystical about girls. They dragged at his eager and longing heart—these roguish-eyed maidens. Not any particular one, but many!

Lorry went to a party one night which was attended by all his school mates. Reluctant, yet tingling, he found himself one of a circle of flush-faced boys and girls, seated around the parlor. The girl for whom the party has been given stood in the center of the room, holding a pillow. She was shy yet provocative. Her dark eyes beamed with coquettish speculation as she glanced from boy to boy to decide upon which her fancy would fall. Whispers and merry laughs and deliberate calls did not embarrass her. At last she selected the boy whom she meant to honor, and casting the pillow at his feet she knelt before him. He plumped down on his knees and gave her a hearty kiss. Blushing, she got up and fled to her seat. The boy then took the pillow and made his choice. So the game began.

Lorry had sustained a shock when this first kiss was exchanged. It might have been him. It was not impossible that as the game progressed some girl would choose him. Then he realized that catastrophe was inevitable. Lorry wanted to run, yet he felt chained there. The atmosphere was enchanting. Laughter and smiles, flashing eyes, rosy cheeks—the strangeness of boy and girl kneeling on the floor, lips to lips—these things seemed incredibly beautiful and mystical to Lorry. He grew excited. An oppression began to weigh upon his breast.

A slip of a girl—Alice Fall—got the pillow, and turned as if her mind had been made up before—to smile sweetly and archly at Lorry. She was in his class at school and he had scarcely ever spoken to her. Alice took a few timid steps toward him. She halted, hugging the pillow. How slim and girlish in her white dress! Lorry had never before noticed that she had great grave hazel eyes and red lips.

"Lorry," she said shyly, and dropping the pillow at his feet she knelt before him with face upturned.

The moment was somehow terrible for Lorry. His heart came up in his throat. He felt blood rush over him. He heard the laughter of the girls and the snicker of the boys. Their faces were dim. But Alice's shone like a flower. Swift was the clash of Lorry's emotions, but even more swift was his realization that here, for the girl's sake, he must not mind. He fell off the chair on his knees and kissed Alice's red lips timidly, fearfully, but swiftly. She bounced up with scarlet face and ran for her seat.

Slowly Lorry arose without the pillow. Suddenly he dashed out of the circle of dim faces, out of the room and out of the house into the dark cool night. A peal of merry laughter followed him, ringing in his ears. Lorry hated it, he hated that stupid, impossible game, yet Alice's kiss burned like sweet fire on his lips. He walked home in the moonlight, under the maples, thoughtful, brooding, now sad, and again exalted. His mother heard him come upstairs and she called: "Aren't you home early, Lorry?"

"Yes—I ran away," he replied haltingly. "They played that game Pillow—and I—,"

He did not conclude his reply, and going to the back room where he and Homer slept he undressed in the dark and went to bed. Homer was fast asleep. Lorry crept close to him, feeling a vague sense of comfort and protection. How dark the room! And it seemed to have moving shadows and noiseless voices. Lorry had once been in the habit of covering his head at night for fear of these things in the dark. He no longer yielded to that cowardice, yet the fears were as strong and inexplicable as ever. Why had Alice Fall chosen him? In all his life she had been the first girl to kiss him. The fact of it was tremendous, the significance beyond his understanding.

Another day Lorry went to a picnic at Grant's Park—a beautiful woods full of chestnut and oak trees, with a shady slope that ran down to the mouth of Timber Run. It was a different crowd of boys and girls from those who had attended the party. Most of them were older. The boys were wilder, the girls freer. They danced instead of playing games. Then they paired off to stroll away in the woods. Lorry liked this better. A strong glamour surrounded these girls, and he seemed to revel in it without fear of ridicule or shame at himself.

There was an unusually attractive girl at this picnic, Maud by name, fifteen years old, shapely and graceful in her tight-fitting dress of blue, with a pretty face and audacious eyes to match. Lorry had seen her many times at school. She was in a lower grade. On this occasion she appeared to single him out with her glances. He met her and danced with her, after which they walked away from the pavilion, out into the shade of the woods. Lorry had never known any one like this girl. She stormed his heart. When they returned to the others, now seated about the picnic dinner on the grass, Lorry felt a strange happiness in her presence.

But soon he was to lose it, as well as her company. Some other boy claimed her, and, roguish and coy, she went with him. After that Lorry watched her, with this rival, then with others. He was to learn the bitterness of jealousy. She was a flirt. She acted precisely the same with them as she had with him. Lorry wandered away under the trees. He felt a restlessness in his body, a fever in his blood. This company of girls, bewildering and sweet as it was, did not satisfy like fishing beside a running stream.

Old Muddy Miser and Dillon's Falls loomed up beside the parties and picnics. There was a struggle in Lorry's mind. He wanted to give up the girls forever, but something warned him to compromise. He would go to the woods and the streams, to the old fisherman and that stretch of white and green water running so swiftly over the yellow rocks. By the time school opened again—a still glorious vast number of days ahead—he would have forgotten what ailed him now.

The next day was the twenty-first of June, the longest day of the year. Bright and early, before Homer was awake, Lorry started out on the road to Dillon's Falls. He was not merely going fishing with the wonderful old fisherman. An unknown future called to Lorry. This walk was a march into life. His step was buoyant, and the miles of dusty road were nothing. There were fields of waving green corn on one side of the road, meadows of red clover on the other. Before Lorry realized he was near the Falls, there loomed the old gray covered bridge. He ran down the short turn off the main road.

The loose boards rattled under his hurried feet. How eagerly he peered through the first knot-hole! Rich and thick the June light, clear and green the swirling water, flashing the golden flat rocks and the bars of gravel! The falls roared a low sweet welcome. It filled his ears with melody. He gazed long, from the green channel beneath the bridge to Big Rock, and up the many white benches of the falls to the narrow level where the river turned between wooded banks. The old fisherman was not in sight.

Lorry kept to the road and passed through a farm, and came at last to the high rocky bluff that formed the west bank of the falls. Sycamore and maples and oaks grew thickly, yet there were openings in the foliage through which he could see the water. Here it ran smooth and swift and green; there it was swirling in deep dark narrow channels; in another place it foamed white over low ledges. This was farther up than Lorry had ever been. He was entranced. He had noticed that the water was low, yet it roared in a way to thrill him and make him wonder how he could ever wade there.

At last he came to the end of the road and to an old dilapidated hut on the bank of the stream. It was made of logs, and was covered with rough-hewn shingles, mossy and green with age. The front of this cabin was open, like a porch, with heavy timbers supporting the roof. The floor was gray clay. A round box in the center with shaft like a wagon-tongue attached to it, and a great quantity of old broken clay pots told Lorry at once that this was the pot-shop where the fisherman lived.

Lorry saw a stone fireplace with ashes still smouldering, and an old skillet and black coffee-pot, and some rude shelves upon which stood a few utensils and bags and cans of food supplies. A door led into the large dark room of the pot-shop. It smelled musty and dank and was empty save for piles of broken clay pots. Lorry spied a wide board over his head that reached from the ground up to a door in the attic above. He mounted it. He looked in upon a loft, well-lighted by holes in the roof and bare, except for some ragged bed-coverings spread upon straw in one corner. This was where the old fisherman slept.

Lorry went down and through the lower part of the shop and came out upon a ledge of rock that projected over a dark green pool, swirling, and spotted with white flecks of foam. Sycamore trees shaded both ledge and pool. Suddenly Lorry spotted Old Muddy Miser standing ankle deep in the water. Lorry opened his lips to call eagerly of his arrival when something made him mute.

The old fisherman swept up a thin straight reed with which he was fishing. Out of the water splashed a shining wiggling chub. Round his head the fisherman swung it to the full length of the line, round and round, half a dozen times. Lorry's amazed gaze saw the chub stop its wiggling and grow limp. It was drunk or dizzy. Then Mr. Miser walked toward a bucket that rested upon a dry stone, all the time swinging the little fish round his head. Slowly he ceased the swinging motion, ending it so the chub hung directly over the open bucket. It made a wiggle and slipped off the hook. Whereupon the fisherman waded back to the spot where he had been fishing.

Lorry now saw that the thin pole was a straight mustard weed, very light and stiff. The line was the thinnest of thread. Lorry could not tell what kind of bait was on the hook, but he certainly saw that it was very small. The old fisherman cast with a quick whipping motion, far from him, into a shallow swift rill, where the water ran over roughened rocks. He let the bait float down with the current. Lorry's keen sight caught the flash of silver, then a splash as a little fish hit the hook, to be jerked out summarily. It too was swung round and round the fisherman's head, and presently held over the open bucket, into which it flopped.

"He's catchin bait," said Lorry to himself. "His hook hasn't any barb, and he swings them dizzy, so they won't get off. . . . Never touches them with his hands! . . . . . Well, if that isn't the slickest thing I ever saw?"

CHAPTER IV

Lorry saw the old fisherman catch more than a dozen chubs and shiners before being discovered.

"Hey! Here you are," shouted the old man.[1] "Welcome as May flowers!"

"Hello, Mr. Miser," returned Lorry, thrilled with the fact that he had been looked for. Swiftly he took off his shoes, and then followed a little path through the brush to a point above the rocky ledge, and down to the level of the water. He waded in boldly. There were swift little channels to cross, where the bottom was rough and footing insecure. Soon, however, he got out upon smooth flat rock, where the water was shallow, and hurried to meet the outstretched hand of the old man.

"Well, Lorry, I've been looking for you these many days," he said.

"I—I couldn't just quite make it," stammered Lorry.

"You got here finally, and now you must come often, especially later in the summer when the bass bite best. . . . I saw you nearly fall as you waded out. You must be careful. After high water the rocks are covered with slime. It's as slippery as slippery elm. Push your feet ahead of you over the rocks and rub off the slime before you trust yourself to step. You'll learn quickly. You're a sturdy lad. But I've had some mighty hard falls. Only last week I hooked a bass out there and forgot to be careful. I slipped—and the bass is there yet for us to catch."

"Was he a big one?" asked Lorry, eagerly.

"Biggest kind of bass. Six pounds easy."

"Did you see him?"

"Saw him take my bait. It was one of these blue chubs[2] I'm catching

---

[1]According to ZG's unpublished autobiography, Old Muddy Miser was 77 years old on their first joint fishing trip.
[2]This common name is unknown today.

now. Best bait for bass. Lively and strong. You hook one through the lips carefully, and the hook holds, but doesn't kill."

"I watched you catch a good many before you saw me. It was just wonderful. I thought I was a minnow-catcher. But—I guess I've worlds to learn."

"A fisherman can learn all his life," replied the old man. "Not only how to find and catch all kinds of fish, but to understand nature, and the beauty and mystery of the life God has created on earth."

These words sank deep into Lorry's heart. Old Muddy Miser, despite the reputation of pauper and hermit and outcast accorded him, despite his rags and the apparent wreck of his life, loomed up greatly to Lorry.

And just then the long stiff mustard reed twitched, and the old man jerked out of the green current a wriggling chub that shone blue and white in the sun. Lorry heard the line whistle as the old fisherman swung the chub round his head and waded over to the bucket. The chub was almost stiff with dizziness and had to be lowered into the bucket before it would shake off.

"Lorry, a real fisherman must be adept at catching bait," said the old man, returning to his post. "It takes as much patience and skill as fishing for the large fish. Look at this hook. It was made from a needle. I took out the temper, bent it suitably with a slight offset. For bait I use the tail of a small hellgramite. It stays on the hook. A piece of worm is just as good bait for minnows but you must put on a fresh piece after every catch. You see my pole is quite long, very light and stiff. The single thread is about eighteen inches longer than the pole. There's a tiny piece of lead a few inches above the hook. This is the best kind of rig for minnows that I have learned to use. . . . Now, watch. I cast quarteringly up and across this shallow swift place. Just a few inches of water there. You'd not expect to find chubs in so shallow a riffle. But they hide behind stones, waiting for feed. You see how the bait drifts, as lightly as thistledown. But it should be under an inch or so. Therefore the bit of lead. You see the chub strike like a little tiger. And you must jerk at the same instant. . . . There! That one was too quick! I'll cast again. Watch. See the bait drifting. There! See that silver shiner with blue fins. He's after it. . . . Another miss! . . . Aha! There's a good big chub. And out he comes."

But in swinging this chub, which was fully ten inches long, the old fisherman threw it off the hook.

"Too big except for the biggest kind of a bass," said the old man. "Now, Lorry, you take the pole, and let's see how apt a pupil you are."

What wonderful little tackle, Lorry thought! It was so easy to handle. The pole was nothing but a weed with a pithy center. It had been dried and was as light as a feather. Lorry made a cast at which the old fisherman nodded approval. Lorry felt that somehow a great deal depended upon how well he acquitted himself. Never had he been so keen and tense to imitate what he had observed in another. He cast and he watched the tiny bait float down. No boy had a sharper eye than Lorry. On the sixth cast he saw a glint of blue, a little swirl back of his bait. Like a flash he jerked, too quickly he thought. But there came an instant when the pole felt a tug, a resistance, lively and strong, and then out of the water splashed a wiggling chub. Lorry swung it out and up, and then round his head, careful to keep the line taut. He watched the chub stop wiggling, grow limp, and straight. Still swinging it over his head, Lorry waded over to the bucket and cautiously let the little fish down, just over the bucket. The chub gave a gasp, and a kick, and slid off the hook.

"Oh, what fun!" exclaimed Lorry, going back. "It's just as fine—takes just as much skill—as big fishing."

"Lorry you will make a great angler," replied the old man. "I see that in you. And by great, I do not mean one who merely catches fish. Once you seize upon the something that cannot be put in words you will understand what I mean. Do not let anyone blind you to the dignity and worthiness of fishing. Christ's best disciples were fishermen. Whatever you give from yourself to fishing—whatever you find in it—will have an incalculable effect upon your life. You will become somebody some day. Not that I mean success in life is the only coveted thing. He also serves who only stands and waits. . . . I came of a good family. Your father will tell you that. I was rich and respected. I lost wealth, position, family, friends—not from wickedness or selfishness on my part. Now I am old and poor—Pogie, as that boy called me—but I find contentment in fishing. And it is going to make me happy to teach you all that it means to me."

Lorry was so astonished he could scarcely conceal his feelings. How utterly incongruous this old man's dignity and eloquence in contrast with his name of outcast, his appearance of a tramp. What little people knew! Lorry's heart warmed to this old fisherman who wanted to help him grow to be good and useful, to make something out of himself.

"Yes sir—I—I think I understand you—sir," he faltered. "I'll do my best to learn to fish—or anything—and I'll never forget."

"Good! I knew the day you licked young Tomans you were a lad after my heart," replied the old man. "Now you go back to the pot-shop and find my other minnow pole. It's on pegs along the wall."

How blue the sky! The waters roared low and musically down the narrow channels. Yet, though a strange rapture grew upon him, it seemed counteracted by a sadness, too deep to understand. He knew he was sorry for Old Muddy Miser. But perhaps that sorrow was ill-placed. The old fisherman was not what he appeared to the callous people who saw and imagined what was not true. Something big awakened in Lorry, vague and undefined.

"Lorry, you will find hellgrammites under flat stones in swift shallow water," instructed the old man when Lorry got back to him. "I lay stones in likely places for traps. Never fail to find one or two. You must stand below the rock you lift. Hellgrammites sometimes let go their hold, roll up and float away."

Lorry had before caught hellgrammites, but early in the spring under stones in the sand. They were white then and very soft, and not like that one the old man showed him. Lorry began lifting flat stones, and the first few hellgrammites he saw drifted away from him in the swift water. The next one that rolled up and began to float Lorry clutched swiftly, heedless of being pinched. And he quickly became acquainted with the sharp pincers. Blood flowed freely from the wound. Lorry retaliated by pulling off the head of the hellgrammite; then doing likewise with the extreme end of the tail, he baited his hook and began to cast for minnows. He tried little pools, runways, rills, holes, and shallow ripples before he found a place where he had a strike. Then he settled down to the earnest joy of conquest, to the thrill of a new game, to the mastering of something that was vastly more than what appeared on the surface.

Chub after chub he missed; he threw this one off and jerked the hook away from that one. Nevertheless, now and then he did make a catch. The blue and white-finned shiners, however, were mostly too swift and clever for him. Still he always saw them strike, and he derived some consolation from his quick sight.

Time seemed to stand still. How amazed Lorry was to hear the old fisherman call that it was noon and lunch hour! They waded ashore. The old man fastened the perforated lid on the bucket and submerged it in a rut in the rock, where swift clear water ran.

"We always catch more bait than we need," he said. "Because it's fun, I suppose. After we eat, we'll try for bass."

Lorry had not forgotten to coax his mother to put up an extra fine lunch, which she had done, plainly curious over his mysterious eagerness. And now, when they had reached the shade of the pot-shop, Lorry was to experience the added pleasure of seeing the old fisherman fry a bass he had caught and dressed that morning.

"You want a good hot fire, burned down so it doesn't blaze," demonstrated the old man. "Heat your skillet hot. Salt and pepper your fish well. Then fry in butter very quickly. It should not take five minutes. But you must watch closely, and turn your fish when it's nicely brown."

Lorry fancied he had never tasted anything as delicious as that fried bass. It pleased him to see how the old fisherman enjoyed the good things from the lunch basket. That noon hour in the shade of the pot-shop fixed the friendship so strangely begun. No longer did Lorry see Old Muddy Miser's rags or remember the stigma attached to his name.

"Fishing for black bass is fine sport," remarked the old man after they had finished eating. "I've read much of salmon and trout, and of the strange fish of the seas. Perhaps there are gamer and more beautiful fish in the world than our bronze-backed, red-eyed, small-mouthed bass. But I don't like to think so. Often I have thought how wonderful it would be to go fishing everywhere—in lakes and streams, in rivers, in the mountains and on the seas. That would be a glorious life. But I never get any farther than dreams—and old Dillon's Falls. . . . Now, you, Lorry, have all your life to live, and if you choose you can catch the lordly salmon and the aristocratic trout, and the fierce fishes of the Seven Seas.[3] I wish I could live to have you tell me about them. . . . You must make fishing a study, a labor of love.

"Don't drink. Most fishermen drink, and many are drunkards. It seems to me they go fishing to find time and place, or earn money to drink whiskey."

"I shall never drink," Lorry replied earnestly. "Last winter, on my birthday—I signed a pledge, and got my brother to do so. You know Francis Murphy, the Evangelist, was in Hainesville holding meetings. My older brother Cedric drinks. And it hurt my mother. So I signed the pledge and got Homer to sign, too. We shall never drink."

"Good!" the old man said and gripped Lorry's hand. He seemed strongly moved. Lorry had vague remembrance of rumor in regard to drink somehow relating to Muddy Miser. "The bottle has had strange power over men of all races," continued the old man. "There is only one other evil thing in life, lad, and that is woman. Bad woman! Perhaps I should say good woman made evil by men. There are fundamentally no bad women. They are mothers of the race. But men are their enemies. You must have a noble ideal of womanhood."

Lorry drank in the old fisherman's words. More than fisherman he was a sage! Old and wise and sad! When he spoke of woman as bad, Lorry experienced a singularly alarming and yet exciting tremor over all his being. The mysterious veil of life hid so much. His knowledge was vague. He had seldom listened to the vile talk of the elder boys and the wondering repetitions of his comrades. Yet Lorry had never been satisfied by parents or teachers. He thirsted for knowledge that did not offend.

---

[3]In Zane Grey's unpublished autobiography, Old Muddy Miser made much more of the "fierce fishes of the Seven Seas" and suggested that young Pearl would someday be the first man to catch many of these giant and unknown species. Of course, this suggestion is heavily colored by Zane Grey's hindsight, and it is apparent from the earlier autobiographical *Fisherman* that in the mid-1920s, "the lordly salmon and the aristocratic trout" were still as much a part of ZG's angling ambition as the tuna and billfish he was catching every summer off Catalina Island.

How impossible to think of sweet-lipped Alice Fall as bad! Yet some day she would be a woman. Then into his mind flashed the face of Maud, brazen, yet somehow irresistible. She too would grow to woman's estate. There were, then, two kinds of women, all growing up from girls. The thought was troublesome and he dismissed it.

"Let's have your fishing pole," said the old man, "and we'll see how you're rigged. . . . Well, well, not so poor for a lad! That pole will be rank poison for bass. But your line is not strong enough for the biggest kind. Your hook is too small, your lead too heavy. Now we will change hook and leader anyway. You must get a heavier line for the next time. For I know where there are some big bass—the biggest kind."

"How big?" asked Lorry, his eyes wide.

"Six pounds—some of them seven," replied the old man. "It'll be better for you to practice on some small ones. Then in August when the corn is ripe we will go after the big fellows."

Lorry watched the old fisherman while he cut off the hook, and replaced it with one twice as large. He looped it on carefully with three half hitches and tried its strength repeatedly. Next he cut a narrow strip of thin lead and rolled it about the line, perhaps a foot above the sinker. He laid the line on a board and rolled the sinker with a flat stone. When completed the slender roll of lead was scarcely larger than the line.

"It's too early in the afternoon, but we'll go anyway," said the old man. "There are a good many small bass on the falls now. I'll show you several places where you can always catch one. I never fail, even when I try them every day. . . . You follow me and do everything I do."

Thus Lorry was launched upon a new adventure. How alluringly bright and beautiful the face of nature—the kingdom of youth—the calling future!

In wading over the rocks after the old fisherman, Lorry found his greatest difficulty arose from impetuosity. He simply could not go slowly. Therefore he slipped and slid and sat down more than once. Some places were easy, others hard, and there were deep swift channels that showed no safe place to set a foot. But the old man knew where to wade, and Lorry gazed at these places with a registering eye. At this upper quarter of the long stretch of rock-bottomed creek there were no falls, but the water ran swiftly and wildly enough to raise a melodious roar. Channels, varying in depth, alternated with flat rock a few inches under the surface. Here and there were holes of different sizes and shapes.

The old fisherman selected a long, deep, narrow channel to try first. Lorry watched him hook a chub delicately through the lips and cast it with easy swing as far as the line would permit up the channel. The bait sank and floated down with the current, past the shelving corners of rock where the dark green depths looked so alluring. Then Lorry baited likewise and selecting another channel of the same characteristics, he imitated as nearly as possible his old teacher's method. He was hard put to watch his line and the old man's, too, but somehow he accomplished both.

"Business!" called the old fisherman.

Lorry had seen the old man's line stop and then cut through the water. He had realized that was a bite before the old man had spoken. The bass ran perhaps twenty feet. Then the old fisherman, extending and lowering the pole, bent forward until he reached as far as possible, when he gave a quick, hard, upward jerk. He hooked the bass. It made a rush, leaped to show itself to be a nice fish of a pound or more in weight, and then ran up the channel, then down. The old man played it carefully, without concern or hurry, and when it had become exhausted, he drew it out of the channel into shallow water, where he caught and unhooked it, and secured it on a string tied to the bucket.

Presently Lorry had a fine strike, but lost his bait through no fault of his own. A pugnacious bass just tore off the chub. He tried another bait in the same place to no avail. Gradually the old fisherman worked downstream towards where a wide still pool stretched from the left bank clear across to the right, and a large channel, having been reinforced by a number of others, poured a tumult of water into this deeper place. When they reached it, the old man set down the bait bucket in six inches of water and began to wade out into the gradually deepening pool. He beckoned to Lorry to follow. They got to a depth over their knees.

"I've been saving this place," said the old fisherman, with an air of great importance. "It's one of my favorites. Haven't tried it for days. There'll be fish here, maybe a big one. . . . Now it takes a long cast. There's a hole under that shelf of rock. See where the water runs fast. Now look at the dark hole. The water swirls a little and runs under the ledge there. That hole goes far back. I've never found how far, though I've stuck a pole in full length. It's a regular cave. Catfish there, too, big mud-cats, which we can get at night. . . . Now pull out all the line you can manage, and swing your bait sideways, far as you can—then forward, to make it drop just where it will drift into that hole. Maybe it won't have to drift."

Lorry essayed most carefully and deliberately to comply with his guide's instructions, but he fell short of the desired spot by several feet.

"Aha! See that!" shouted the old man.

Indeed Lorry had noticed a golden flash and a swirl. How he tingled!

CHAPTER V

Lorry's several attempts at casting the next bait were similar to his first, but at last he placed the chub right at the dark cleft that yawned so enticingly. A bass broke water, taking his bait. Lorry waited until the line had stretched taut, then he jerked hard. He felt the instantaneous surge on his pole, and then the release of strain as the bass came up. How he leaped—fully three feet into the air! Gold and black he looked and he

shook himself like a tussling dog. Four times he came out and then darted away to the right, whizzing line off the reel, and working into the swift channel. He was only a pound bass, but he made a valiant battle for life. Lorry was long in besting him; and he discovered when he tied the beautiful mottled fish to the bucket, that his fingers were all thumbs.

After this success he had five more strikes, casting from the identical spot, and of these he captured two bass, the largest a pound and a half. That appeared to exhaust this hole. They waded out and around, and to other places lower down. One spot in particular struck Lorry as being a most wonderful hiding place for bass. It was well over toward the left bank, a cleft in the rocks, fed by rushing white-bubbled channels, with deep water under a submerged log. The old fisherman called this place Sycamore Hole. The water appeared to be foamy, then green and swift, and finally, as it neared the sunken log, deep and dark and golden. But this marvelous place did not yield a strike. The old man expressed surprise and disappointment. "There's a big one in here, only he's not hungry." They turned back then and worked up the left bank of the stream, where Lorry found precarious wading. He skinned his shin. Channels were many, deep and swift, with only a narrow rim of rock between. The slime on the rock was more treacherous there than on the other side. Lorry caught three more bass and a huge goggle-eye, a black-spotted species of sunfish.[1]

"Well, Lorry, if you're to get home by dark you must go," said the old man.

Lorry was as amazed as he was miserable to find that the day had flown. The sun was setting. Where had the hours gone? What a glorious day! They waded across at the head of the falls, back to the old pot-shop.

"Lad, you'll come again?" queried the old fisherman.

"Come—again!" laughed Lorry, with a break in his voice, "Indeed I shall. . . . But I couldn't thank you enough for this day. Good-bye."

That was the beginning of a changed life for Lorry Dunn. Three days a week he journeyed to Dillon's Falls to fish with Old Muddy Miser. No one discovered his treasured secret. Most manfully he resisted the temptation to exhibit the bass he caught to the Graves boys. Homer was sworn to silence in regard to Lorry's fishing fortunes. Only his mother knew where he went.

The other days, on three of which he had to work, and on Sunday go to Sunday School and church, were nightmares of endurance. Yet no one

---

[1] A goggle-eye, redeye, or northern rock bass (*Ambloplites rupestris*) is "huge" at 15 inches and weighing more than 2 pounds.

guessed his hatred of confinement. Lorry was not without gratitude, nor lacking in a sense of duty. Never had sweeping his father's office or grinding and polishing sets of false teeth—for his father was a dentist— seemed so insupportably hideous. So, with these labors, and mowing the lawn, a task consigned to Homer but which he absolutely would not do, Lorry had to waste three precious days each week.

As for Sunday School—that had come to be an irksome duty. He never knew the lessons, and his teacher said it was not stupidity but simply that he was a lazy bad boy, and would surely live to be hanged. Lorry did not share her conviction. Still he was ashamed that he could not put his attention on Sunday School tracts, or stay awake in church. Lorry could have listened if the preacher had told a story, or at least something interesting. But he always harangued about people's sins and hell, which were things that did not greatly concern Lorry.

July passed and hot summer fell upon the Muskingum valley. The dreaded "dog-days" came in August along with the golden rod and the locusts. Stagnant ponds grew a green scum upon them, where the "snake-feeders" or dragonflies wheeled and the frogs sunned themselves upon lily-pads. Licking Creek fell low, until many were the bare flats and ledges of rock on Dillon's Falls. Hot as a stove, almost, were these sun-baked rocks to the bare foot. The water lost something of its cool quality and appeared to thicken, yet Lorry failed to feel any ill effects from continual wading in it.

Lorry's store of fishing knowledge was continually increasing. He did not see how he could remember all he had learned and was learning. If there were a thousand channels and rifts for black bass on the falls, Lorry learned to know them all; if there were ten thousand ripples and pockets and shoals where the minnows lurked, Lorry had fished them all. He could wade across the falls at any point. What boy but he could do that? Lorry knew there was no other and he was proud. Wild horses could not have dragged from him the disclosure of secret places revealed to him by Old Muddy Miser. Often lads and men came to fish at the falls, but never, even by accident did they drop a bait into one of these secret favorite recesses, where there was always a hungry bass waiting.

Lorry adopted the names given by the old fisherman to these places, and, in fact, to all parts of the stretch of rocks and currents from Big Rock to the pot-shop. Like music to Lorry were these names—Head of Falls— Pot-shop Pool—Big Channel—The Long Hole—Shady Rift— Sycamore Hole—and so on down the steps and inclines of the falls to the sand-bars and islands at the foot.

Most wonderful of all, Lorry had caught bass every day that he had fished, either alone or with the old man. Sometimes the old man would rest, or mend tackle, or go to sell some fish he had caught, during which hours Lorry would occupy himself alone. He had hooked several large bass, but they had outwitted or out-pulled him. Always he knew that one day he was going to get hold of one of the big bass. So thrilling, so poignant was this assurance, that he was loth to have it happen soon. He hugged the thought; he dreamed of it.

Many other kinds of fish fell to Lorry's growing skill—rock bass,[2] calico bass,[3] goggle eyes, mud-cats, blue-cats, channel cats, and several varieties of suckers. The blue-cats were rare,[4] and seldom hooked. Once, while standing in swift water, fishing far down, Lorry hooked so heavy a fish that he could not hold it. But it rolled on the surface, a huge blue-cat, with enormous mouth, blue in color as the sky. It took all his line off the reel and then broke away. Lorry grieved at the loss of that fish. Many an hour he stood in the same spot, with swift water tugging at his legs and tiny minnows nibbling at his toes, in the hope of again hooking that big blue-cat. But in vain.

It was great fun to fish for the calico bass. This had to be done, if successfully, very early in the morning. The old fisherman sometimes located a school of these thin oval-shaped calico-speckled bass, of silvery and pearly hue, and would have ready a bucketful of tiny minnows for bait when Lorry arrived. These fish were always taken in eddies below the falls. A piece of cornstalk was slit and slipped on the line, ten feet above the lead, to be used as a float or bobber. It was fun for Lorry when a calico bass took one of the small minnows, to see the cornstalk nod and sail away, and suddenly flop under. These fish seldom ran as high as a pound in weight and had nothing of the savage gameness of the black bass, yet they afforded much sport, and were very good to eat.

Above the falls on both sides of the creek were lines of heavy timber, sycamore, maples, willows and cottonwoods. Between this border-fringe of woods and tall green cornstalks, Lorry and the old fisherman wore a well-beaten trail. In late August as the corn ripened, slowly turning to

---

[2]Since Zane Grey lists goggle-eye separately, this "rock bass" is probably the look-alike warmouth bass (*Lepomis gulosus*) which is still abundant in lakes, ponds and smaller rivers south and east of the Great Lakes. However, because its maximum size in Ohio is only about 8 inches, it has never been as popular a recreational fish as the other "goggle-eye."

[3]Calico bass is a regional name for the black crappie (*Pomoxis nigro-maculatus*).

[4]Thanks largely to dams, the blue or great forktail catfish (*Ictalurus furcatus*) is today quite rare in the Ohio River drainage. This species is migratory, moving upriver and into tributaries during the summer months and moving downstream and south with the advent of cold weather. Like all catfishes, the blue is most active at night or on overcast days, and exceptional specimens reach weights in excess of 100 pounds.

gold, they took to fishing deeper water. Bartlett's Run flowed into the creek a mile above the falls, and below this junction there was a ledge of rock extending halfway across. It ended abruptly in deep water. Here was one of Muddy Miser's favorite holes for bass of the biggest kind, and was at its best after sundown on quiet evenings. Often they went there, and caught bass, but not yet had Lorry seen or felt one of the big fellows.

When they fished this place, which they called Cottonwood Ledge, they always went up Bartlett's Run to catch bait, and this in itself was a happy event for Lorry. Bartlett's was very different from Joe's Run. It was wild and unfrequented and ran between high grassy banks, and had deep holes full of the hungriest and biggest chubs Lorry had ever seen. He could stand in one spot, and casting from a bank over a swift riffle that ran into a deep hole, catch a chub or shiner at every cast. Many a time he had caught fifty out of one hole.

Above Dillon's Falls on the other side from Bartlett's there was a sheltered pond of deep water that was strongly fresh, probably fed from springs at the bottom. It was perhaps a mile from the pot-shop, by way of a path trodden through a long cornfield. This pond was the old fisherman's best place to catch the rarest bait for bass—a golden shiner.[5] Lorry loved to go there. The walk through the rustling cornstalks, the hidden nature of the pond nestled under high-wooded banks, flower-skirted and bird-haunted, the turtles sunning themselves on logs, the water-snakes gliding down through the moss and ferns, and the illusive, golden-sided, tender-mouthed shiners, so difficult to catch—these things made the place grow dear to Lorry. No one else knew of it. The farmer who owned the land called it a bog-hole, and had never been down to it; the other fisher boys passed it by.

CHAPTER VI

These shiners were strange finicky little fish. Not always would they bite, and nothing but angle worms would tempt them. Tiny hooks and tiny baits had to be used, and the fisherman must keep out of sight. Like brook trout rising to flies these golden shiners broke water after the deceptive bait. Usually they were large, and all of them were strong, exceedingly active, and full of fight. The high bank made it necessary to

[5]Although ZG makes much of the spring-fresh quality of the pond where Old Muddy Miser caught his golden shiners (*Notemigonus crysoleucas*), this species can survive in oxygen-depleted waters that would suffocate most other fishes. For this reason, golden shiners are today one of the most common live baits sold in tackle stores throughout the midwest, and the annual retail value of golden shiners reared in Missouri alone is approximately $2 million.

swing them up, and this fact, coupled with the other difficulties, made the capture of one out of five hooked a fortunate average. Also they were hard to keep alive. Fresh water had to be supplied frequently.[1] Lastly, if one of these shiners was dropped alive and wiggling into a hole where there was a bass, he was almost sure to take it.[2]

Not until these happy all-satisfying days were over and September with the waning of summer was at hand and school imminent did Lorry realize just how much the days had meant to him. And not until the very last day did he summon courage to tell his friend that he could come no more this year.

"All play and no work make a bad boy, Lorry," said the old fisherman. "You must study. Summer is over. But the May flowers will bloom again. I will be here next spring. And Dillon's Falls will always be here."

So they parted, and Lorry went home with an ache in his heart. Soon it was as if Dillon's Falls were a dream.

High school opened many avenues of new interest to Lorry, but the splended average in studies that he had maintained in the Eight Ward school did not here materialize. It was not that Lorry was not keen to advance. He started in with ambition. But soon he was thrown into companionship with new and more attractive girls, who made eyes at him and wrote notes to him and waited for him after school. This popularity incurred the disfavor of some of the other boys and also that of Lorry's teacher. She was a large, severe-faced, sharp-tongued woman, who showed little evidence of remembering that she had once been young. Lorry was singularly sensitive to praise or blame; and about this time he discovered that he was also subject to spells of depression. Altogether these distractions operated against Lorry's applying himself, and at the end of the term some of his marks were poor.

This fact distressed him, and he set about manfully to make up for it. But circumstances were against him. Blame for some prank involving a girl was unjustly laid upon Lorry. He could not tell the truth without hurting the girl. Following that came an unfortunate occurrence. Lorry

---

[1] Although golden shiners can exist in low-oxygen environments, they cannot abide overcrowding as well as some other, less active minnows. Furthermore, while some of the dace and other minnows that ZG caught and put in his bucket were large at three inches, golden shiners are frequently five and six inches long. ZG's fond reminiscence about golden shiner fishing puts me in mind of an outing in the Catskills for trout that was only saved from being a blank by a golden shiner fully 9 inches long and probably as many years old since this species grows approximately an inch each summer.

[2] One of the ironies of the bass family's fondness for golden shiners as food is that golden shiners frequently scatter their adhesive eggs over the nests of bass and sunfish. If the spawning shiners get away with this daring act, their eggs and then their young, which hatch about four days after spawning, will be protected by the aggressive male bass or sunfish protecting its own eggs and fry.

had a good clear tenor voice and he liked to sing, but he did not read music well and had no great aptitude for holding a tune. On Fridays, when the professor of music came, two classes were merged into one. Lorry shared a front seat with another youth, a very good singer. At the beginning of the lesson, when the class was in full chorus and Lorry was singing at the top of his lungs, the professor tapped sharply on a desk to command silence. Pointing his stick at Lorry he said: "You keep still!" The boys and girls let out what seemed to Lorry a roar of mirth. He felt the blood burn his cheek and temple. "If I can't sing it's not because I haven't tried," he cried sharply to the professor. "Why haven't you taught me how? You give some of the girls special lessons."

The professor was furious and sent Lorry back to his own classroom. Lorry slammed his music book down, muttering: "I'll never open it again." And indeed he never did. His teacher punished him by keeping him after school hours, made a butt of him before the other pupils, and lectured him, all to no purpose. Lorry was through studying music. At last the matter of his delinquency was laid before his father. Lorry told the truth and proved it by one of his classmates. Dr. Dunn curtly informed the teacher that he did not blame Lorry and upheld him. .

It was a victory for Lorry that turned out badly. It increased his teacher's inclination to dislike him. She had her pets, and one of them was the youth who could sing so well; and he made the mistake of ridiculing Lorry. The result was that this boy with the silver voice went home from school that day with two black eyes.

All these things might have been of little consequence to a boy of different temperament. But Lorry knew he was misunderstood and unappreciated; and gradually something unhappy formed in his mind. It did not soothe his ruffled temper when his father made him go to work Saturdays clerking in a shoe store. From eight o'clock in the morning until eleven at night! Lorry wondered if it were possible to hate anything more! His mother divined his feelings and sought to comfort him, but though this made Lorry love her more, it only added to his shame.

It was a long hard cold winter. Lorry read books when he should have been studying. He was an omnivorous reader. He read everything he could get his hands on, but *Robinson Crusoe* and *The Last of the Mohicans* and the Harry Castlemon books were his favorites. He devoured them. He knew them by heart.

One evening a week he went to a dancing club to which he belonged. His popularity here, at least with the girls, had not waned. If anything, it had increased. Lorry did not have tact, and he was not of a temper to toady to boys or try to propitiate rivals. He danced right on gallantly and to certain disaster.

There were only three girls in this set whom Lorry liked equally when they were all together, and each one best when he was with her separately. He knew his predicament, yet seemed to welcome the coils that closed round him. Effie Wolcott was sixteen, fair-faced, with great eyes like dark velvet; Marjorie Brown a year older, was tall and slim and proud, gray-eyed, with a wonderful braid of golden hair; Elinor Roberts, the same age, small and dark, sad sweet lips and sad eyes. Lorry laid siege to their hearts, without conscious motive, just drawn by youth and beauty and something nameless, of which he had no knowledge.

It so happened that Effie had a brother, a debonnaire, high-handed young fellow, chum of the president of the club, and both hated Lorry. At the height of Lorry's popularity these two conspirators malignantly exaggerated a playful and innocent remark of Lorry's and used it as a means to expel him from the dancing club. The shock to Lorry was terrible. He could not believe it. Protests to the president of the club were unavailing. At last Lorry realized he had been greatly wronged. He was sure the girls had not been let into the secret, because they were unusually sweet and solicitous with inquiries as to why he did not attend the latest club dance. This made his situation only worse. Lorry sought young Wolcott and at length cornered him in his father's store. Lorry told him quick and hard what he was. Young Wolcott sat on a table among his bosom friends, and despite their proximity he turned deathly pale.

"Come outside. I *dare* you to," demanded Lorry fiercely.

"I wouldn't fight with you," replied Wolcott.

"You bet you wouldn't—you coward," retorted Lorry. "All right, this is your time. Mine will come!"

The winter passed, a long bitter time for Lorry Dunn. With the advent of spring, however, he began to lose much of the brooding that had settled upon him, and started to think of summer and Dillon's Falls. As time went on Lorry found that, had he but known, his girl friends would have been glad to see him all through this dark period. He redoubled his former attentions and was more popular than ever. Then it leaked out that he had been expelled from the dancing club, and why. Some of Lorry's friends loyally championed him; they knew he could not be guilty of what he was accused. But Elinor Roberts acted strange and aloof, and Effie Wolcott abruptly grew cold. One night, the last he was ever with her, he took her home from a party on the Terrace. As there was a merry crowd of young people together he did not get a moment alone with her until they reached her home. She went into the yard and closed the gate between them. It was moonlight. Her face was white and beautiful, and her dark eyes gazed up at him. Lorry stammered a few words of appeal. But she bade him goodnight and turned away.

Lorry went home beset by anger and doubt. His blood boiled at the injustice done him, and he lay awake at night beside his brother, pondering and miserable. On Saturday afternoon of that same week he met Marjorie Brown on the street. She looked into his face as if she had never seen him. She did not know him. Lorry, cut to the quick, did not give up without another fight. On Sunday night he went to Marjorie's church and, after the services waited for her outside. Lorry went to his defeat like a soldier. Marjorie came out in company with her family and friends, and Lorry faced her with uncovered head.

"Marjorie, may I walk home with you," he asked quite clearly. "I have something most important to say."

That was a crucial moment in Lorry's life, perhaps in Marjorie's. With deliberate scorn she turned her back.

Lorry took the insult as he would have taken a blow in the face. All the lights seemed to dim. Tears in his eyes! Something of boyhood died in him then. He was ashamed of her, of her sex, of the falseness of her and those who had made her blind. But this nobler emotion gave place to fury. He would show her how little he cared—for her—for anyone. He would show them what a man he was. He would beat Ralfe Wolcott half to death or get drunk. But to drink was impossible. There was the pledge he had signed to please his mother. Still he must find something terrible to do.

Lorry's evil genius kept pace with him. At the corner he met two boys he knew well, both older, and noted for experiences still foreign to Lorry.

"Come on, Lorry. We're going to Jumbo's," said Charlie Hawes and Harvey Stout.

Lorry seemed caught in a current he could not, did not want to resist. His mood was such that what he would have rejected at any other single hour of his life he now embraced. Jumbo. She was a notorious woman who kept a house of ill-fame. Lorry had passed it. He had wondered with all the curiosity of dawning youth. He forgot his mother; he forgot Homer and the faith of Old Muddy Miser. He remembered only Marjorie's scornful face. Very well, he would be what she thought him. Exuberantly, he fell in with these boys and accompanied them.

CHAPTER VII

The leaven of evil was working in Lorry Dunn. But his consciousness for the moment knew only a different kind of thrill, a dark excitation of spirit, the enticing first sensations of forbidden fruit.

The house in question was situated down by the river near the railroad tracks, in a neighborhood that was lonely and dark. Lorry and Harvey followed Charlie Hawes through an alleyway to the rear of the house where Charlie knocked on a door. Lorry held his breath. He seemed to be crossing a threshold into tremendous strife, a raw wildness of unknown forces. On the instant a sudden reluctance and fear assailed him. But it was too late. The door opened.

A tall, blonde, handsome woman, huge of form, welcomed them into a cozy little parlor, warmly tinted and strongly redolent of perfume. Lorry strove to act naturally, but he could not have spoken a word.

"Girls, here's company," called Jumbo, in a mellow pleasant voice.

A young woman entered. Her appearance made Lorry gasp. She was somehow shockingly beautiful. Her face shone white in the lamp-light. She had large wine-dark eyes, under which lay heavy shadows. Her lips appeared too red to be natural. Her hair was auburn, long and wavy. Arms and shoulders and breast were bare, white as snow.

After two steps into the parlor she halted. The hawk-like expression of her eyes changed to astonishment and something too elusive for Lorry to grasp. She wheeled to Jumbo.

"Do you expect us to entertain these kids?" she queried sharply.

"Certainly I do," replied the proprietress, just as sharply.

"I will not do it," protested the other.

A mocking high-pitched laugh pealed from an adjoining room, followed by a rustle of silk.

"Laurie,[1] it's fun to rob the cradle," said a voice that matched the laugh. Then the owner of it entered the parlor. She presented a contrast to the girl called Laurie. Even more scantily clad, she was short and voluptuous, with a baby face and big blue eyes.

"Why, here's my Charlie boy," she trilled.

Just then there came a quick hard knock on the door. Suddenly the parlor was silent as a tomb. The girls stiffened. Manifestly they recognized that knock. It came again, louder.

"Who's there?" demanded Jumbo with her blonde head bent to the door.

"Open in the name of the law! Your house is surrounded!"

"We're pinched!" cried the short girl, gayly.

"Oh, it's tough on these boys!" exclaimed the one named Laurie, and there was genuine distress in her voice.

---

[1] Zane Grey intended that the name of this prostitute (Laurie) and his protagonist (Lorry) be pronounced the same way to hint at the dark paths the boy (i.e., the youthful Zane Grey) might have taken but for the ameliorating influence of fishing.

Jumbo cursed under her breath and then opened the door. Two men strode in. Lorry recognized the first one as Lieutenant Weaver, chief of police. When he espied the boys, he was plainly astonished and disconcerted.

"Weaver, you'll not arrest these boys," asserted Jumbo.

"I've got to do my duty," replied the officer. "How did I know you had some kids here? . . .You'll get a long sentence for this, Jumbo."

She glared and swore at him. Evidently there was enmity between them. The situation was not improved by the fact that Harvey and Charlie began to cry. Lorry was too stunned for any expression of feeling. A revulsion surged over him, and suddenly his legs were weak. Arrested in a house of ill-fame! Then he thought of his mother and Homer and a horrible despairing remorse assailed him. The girl Laurie was looking at him with understanding and sympathetic eyes.

"Weaver, you must not arrest these boys," she begged. "It will mean ruin. Let this be a lesson to them. Take it out on us and let them off."

"Shut up, you hussy! You're a fine one to preach," growled the officer. "Hurry up—get on your hats and coats. . . . Bates, take the women in the patrol-wagon. I'll walk these boys to the station and go the back way."

Before Lorry realized what was happening he was led out into the dark night by Lieutenant Weaver. Charlie and Harvey were in charge of other officers. They disappeared in the gloom.

"Lorry, if your mother finds this out it will half kill her," said the Lieutenant.

"Can't you—keep it—secret?" faltered Lorry.

"I'll do my best. We'll get your fathers over and send for Mayor Ritchie."

"Oh, I could never—thank you enough," replied Lorry. A hope rose in him that it might not turn out so terribly. He was sure no one saw him on the way to the station, and that was added relief. Lorry was led through corridors into the jail, and locked in a cell already occupied by Charlie and Harvey. Both boys appeared more upset than ever; indeed they roused in Lorry a kind of contempt.

"Can't you take your medicine?" he asked, disgustedly, of Charlie Hawes. But Charlie did not raise his head from his hands or cease his moanings. Harvey sat in the corner, utterly dejected and shaken.

Lorry walked to and fro. He felt of the iron cage-like door. Yes, he was locked in a cell. The horror of it! Suddenly a white hand and arm flashed through the grating from the adjoining cell. It grasped Lorry's coat.

"Look here, Lorry," said a voice. Then Lorry realized the girls had been locked in the adjoining cell. By flattening his face against the grating Lorry could see the girl Laurie. "You're a game lad. I'm sorry. You fell in with bad company. . . . I'd like to believe you'll never go into such a house again."

"I—never will,"whispered Lorry, and his thoughts flashed to the old fisherman.

"Keep away from bad women—like me," she went on. "Only ruin can come of it, for such as you. I know."

She squeezed his arm and then let go. The white hand slipped back through the grating. Lorry turned away to sit down on the bench. Was this girl Laurie a bad woman, as she confessed?

It was two o'clock in the morning when the three boys were led from the cell into the dim court-room. Mayor Ritchie sat behind the high desk. Lorry saw his father, pale of face and stern. Harvey's father was there, and Charlie's mother. She had been weeping. In a very few moments Mayor Ritchie had dismissed the boys. Lorry found himself out in the cool gray darkness walking beside his father. He expected a terrible upbraiding and threats of direful punishment, but they were not forthcoming. Gradually it dawned upon Lorry that his father was too deeply shocked to think of punishment. Finally Lorry burst out with his story, without excuse for himself, without a word against the boys who had led him astray.

"Weaver said you'd just got in that woman's house when he came. Was he telling the truth?" replied his father.

"Yes. We hadn't been in there more than two minutes," answered Lorry.

That was the only time his father spoke during the long walk back to the Terrace. The gray of dawn was breaking in the east. Lorry faced his mother with a sense of hateful guilt. She had not been in bed. At sight of him the strained look of worry left her. He told her, as he had told his father. She did not reproach him. Lorry went to his room and crept in beside Homer.

Next day Lorry went to school as usual. No one could have suspected the dread under which he labored. In a few days his fears, and those of his comrades in guilt, were almost lulled. But they felt relieved too soon. Mayor Ritchie gave Jumbo such a hard sentence that the poor woman drank concentrated lye and died in her cell. This focused attention on the arrest and gradually the truth became known. To men about town at first, then to the boys, and lastly to the girls.

Lorry saw his disgrace, his ruin in the averted faces of his old friends. Yet the blow did not make him bow his head. He accepted the fact and resigned himself to it. A coldness and aloofness settled upon him. As far as the boys were concerned his escapade had only enhanced his individuality. Most of them liked him the better. Most of the girls, too, would have stood by him, had he permitted such loyalty. Alice Fall and Bell Dugdale met him with frank open eyes of undefiled faith, but Lorry would have neither their sympathy nor championship. As for the three girls he had loved and who had flouted him before this catastrophe, Lorry passed them at school and on the street as indifferently as if he had been a prince and they of lowly estate. His heart was sore, but they could no longer hurt him. Soon, to his infinite relief, the long vacation came, and Lorry forgot his troubles.

Lorry heard his mother say to his father: "Let the boy out of work in town this summer. It will be better for him to be away from people. Let him fish to his heart's content."

His father was at length persuaded. Lorry's blood leaped with the import of his mother's words, yet somehow they stung. What had he done that he would be better away from people? Disgraced himself! Yet the shame Lorry suffered was not on his own account, but for those whom he had so grievously hurt. Somehow his conscience would not hold him greatly guilty.

So Lorry began his fishing in a strange earnestness. He relied on it for something—he knew not what. But it seemed to be what his mother had hinted. Lorry felt a sweet strong persuasive influence telling him that in fishing all troubles would be alleviated, all perplexing problems levelled, all evils made as if they had not been.

Lorry did not betray even to his mother how really bad his case was. He was not yet sixteen, and he had forced upon him a significance of the battle of life. Lorry accepted it, not resignedly, but with secret passionate revolt. For his mother's sake, for Homer's sake more than all else, because he felt responsible for the boy he resolved to do something great with his life. A second thought wavered hauntingly in his consciousness—he would fool these sarcastic people who gossiped that Lorry Dunn had been born to be hanged. As for those shallow fickle girls—they would live to see the day they would be glad to recognize him. How would he repay them? The dark instinct of revenge stirred in Lorry. But he killed it in its incipiency. "Not for me—not that kind of stuff!" he brooded. "That's for fellows like Ralfe Danis and Billy Fillman. Never for me! . . . I might not forget, but I would return good for evil!"

Lorry had a long talk with Homer, something more kindly and brotherly and persuasive than ever before. The lad seemed singularly responsive. However Lorry advised rather than dominated. And he concluded this harangue with these words: "If you get into a fight, see that you lick the fellow!"

Lorry went to Dillon's Falls to resume the quaint friendship of the preceding summer. He found Old Muddy Miser exactly as he had seen him last; the pot-shop looked the same. Woods and waters smiled the old welcome. Lorry considered long as to whether or not he would confess what had happened to him, and in the end decided not to distress his old friend by an exposure of that miserable story. Lorry was unflinchingly sincere with himself. He felt that if there had been the slightest possibility of his ever erring again in like manner he would tell it and profit by the same. But Lorry knew he had taken his final step in that direction.

Licking Creek was high, and the season early. Fishing for both bait and bass was rather unproductive. Lorry and the old fisherman worked over tackle, and talked, and set great store upon the late summer. Lorry was sure he could persuade his mother to let him camp out at Dillon's Falls with Old Muddy Miser, and that would obviate the long walks to and fro, just at the best fishing hours.

Lorry and Homer were two of the best baseball players in Hainesville, and their services were greatly in demand. What with fish and playing, the days were far too short. Wonderful to see, Homer took care of the mowing of the lawn twice a week, an irksome task the brother despised. Moreover, it seemed needless work. The grass was prettier when allowed to grow long.

One night Crow Graves met Lorry on his way home from an errand.

"Fishin' great at Muskingum Dam," announced Crow. "Today I ketched three salmon an' two perch."

"How big?" inquired Lorry, driving at once for the cardinal issue with fishermen.

"Salmon little. But I had a big one on, an' I seen Dave Hook ketch a twelve pounder,"[2] replied Crow. "He was standin' in the swift place where the mill-race runs out over the rocks, an' fishin' in the white water right under the dam. You oughta seen thet salmon fight. . . . Then I ketched two perch on soft-shell crawfish. Three pounders,[3] too. My uncle Al says there's a run of salmon an' perch. You'd better come with me tomorrow."

"I'd like to go, Crow," replied Lorry, eagerly.

"All right. Get up early an' meet me down there about five o'clock."

CHAPTER VIII

The gray of the following dawn, when all objects were indistinct in the opaque gloom, Lorry strode swiftly down the street under the iron bridge where the railroad crossed and down the steep incline to the rocks below. Crow was waiting for him at the appointed place, pole in hand, minnow-bucket set on the rock. What did Crow's lazy disregard of work and school amount to when he went fishing? He was always on time; he

---

[2]There is some question about what species of fish Crow Graves refers to. Both the walleye (*Stizostedion vitreum*) and sauger (*S. canadense*) are called "jack salmon" in portions of their mostly mid-American range. However, while sauger are more abundant in rivers with a strong current (like the Muskingum) than the walleye, sauger rarely exceed three pounds, although the world record from a North Dakota reservoir was almost 9 pounds in weight. And while the world record walleye from a Tennessee lake weighed 25 pounds, this species rarely achieves weights half that size, and a river-caught walleye normally is huge at 6 pounds. Finally, the common white sucker (*Catostomus commersoni*) was once called "salmon" by midwestern fishermen who canned the species much the way salmon were canned and for one of the same reasons: to soften the fish's many small bones in the pickling or steaming process. However, white suckers seldom take a baited hook and are immense at eighteen inches. Furthermore, they are most often speared or snagged during their spring spawning migration.

[3]If Crow's "salmon" are walleye, then his "perch" are probably yellow perch (*Perca flavescens*). Both these fishes are closely related, they eat minnows, are excellent eating in turn and both provide wonderful recreation. However, just as Crow undoubtedly overestimated the size of the "salmon" caught by Dave Hook, he has certainly exaggerated the size of the perch he caught. The world-record yellow perch weighed slightly more than four pounds and very, *very* few caught beyond tidal water in North America ever weigh more than a pound.

never tired; he shared his best place or lent his pole, and happiest of all, he was as glad to have someone else catch a fine fish as if he caught it himself. Lorry learned early that this was a lovable quality in fishermen. Crow Graves could be mean, but not while he was fishing.

The boys headed out under the old Y bridge, a covered structure crossing the mouth of Licking Creek and the Muskingum and followed a ledge of rock that led under the railroad bridge and beyond to a ledge of slab-like rocks. The air was full of mist from the rapids of the river, and the roar of the tumbling waters was deafening. Cool and fresh and wet blew the winds set in motion by the fall of water.

"Look ahere," shouted Crow, and with his two hands cupped he dipped them in his bucket and lifted a swarm of lively big chubs and shiners. "Ketched them up Joe's Run yesterday."

Crow Graves possessed shifty, hard, blue eyes, but at this moment they glistened with ardor and generosity. "Help yourself, Lorry," he said, "an' let's fish like the devil before any one comes. We beat them here."

Lorry needed no second bidding. The first wiggling bait he dropped into the water was seized by a fish before he had a chance to wade out where he wanted to go. He hooked a lusty bass of two pounds and pulled it out in short order. Crow yelled something, the meaning of which was drowned by the pour of water. Next time Lorry got out to a point of ledge, in swift water up to his knees, and cast his bait out into the green boiling current. He let the bait drift away from him and let out more line. Suddenly he had a quick sharp strike new to him. He missed. Crow saw him miss and waved a tragic hand. Lorry put on another bait and tried again. But soon he had to move back to let Crow pass under his pole, for Crow had hooked a fish and was unceremoniously dragging it along to shallow water in the rock pile. Here he jerked it out—a long, silvery, big-eyed salmon.

That was the beginning of a river fishing experience which almost rivalled Dillon's Falls. Crow, who was impetuous and violent, broke his line on a heavy fish. Lorry caught two nice salmon, and played a large one for fifteen minutes. But it was too strong and clever for him. At the critical time he gave slack line and the fish got away. Then other fishermen began to arrive, until the rocks were lined. This crowd did not appeal to Lorry, but as he and Crow had secured the best places he was able to endure it.

Meanwhile the sun rose bright, and with the business of day, wagons and pedestrians began to cross the bridges. Lorry knew his father often went to town this way, and crossed the railroad bridge. And it chanced that presently Lorry had another swift, sharp strike. The instant he hooked this salmon he knew he had his hands full. The anglers on the rocks below obligingly pulled in their lines to give Lorry a fair field to play his fish. This one was like lightning, and if he had been heavy, he would have bested Lorry. Twice he ran off all the line. Once he headed into the foamy current and went clear to the thundering fall of waters that rolled over the dam. But at last Lorry subdued him, and waded along the ledge toward the rocks, with the long white rolling salmon shining in the sunlight.

Lorry gazed up at the railroad bridge, and there on the board walk stood his father watching him. What a proud moment for Lorry when he landed that four-pound salmon! The morning ended, however, as so many fishing days, with disaster. Lorry hooked something that nearly smashed his pole and did break his line.

"Gee, you're a lucky fellar!" exclaimed Crow Graves.

"Lucky! Do you call that luck?" wailed Lorry, "I've got to quit, my line's gone!"

"What d'ye want for fifteen cents—canary birds?" retorted the practical Crow.

Thereafter, for several weeks, Lorry alternated his fishing trips between Dillon's Falls and Muskingum Dam. His luck at the latter place held so remarkably that he acquired a wonderful reputation among the older fishermen. Lorry felt that he was just applying Muddy Miser tactics on the larger fish of the river. One day he caught a seven-pound mudcat[1] and landed it without help, a feat remarkable in that swift water. Another time he and Crow were seining for minnows up under the apron of the dam in a narrow place that had been broken out by ice. Lorry felt something heavy hit the mosquito-net seine.

"Lift quick!" yelled Lorry.

That was easy to say, but hard to do. A heavy weight dragged in the seine. But up they came with it, to disclose an enormous salmon, wallowing in the bag of the net.

"Roll him up," bawled Crow. "Frantically the two of them staggered together, folding and wrapping the fish. It struggled so hard that it knocked over one and then the other. At last they dragged it to shallow water where they fell upon it and secured it. Fifteen pounds it weighed![2] A lordly fish, silver and white, with dark specks and a rose flush, and

---

[1]While both the black bullhead (*Ictalwus melas*) and flathead catfish (*Pylodictis olivaris*) are known as "mudcats" in various parts of their range, the large size of this fish and, even more so, the one mentioned later on surely designate these cats as flatheads. A bullhead rarely exceeds 3 pounds, but flathead catfish frequently weigh ten times that.
[2]This has to be a walleye—but what a monster for Ohio waters!

huge black eyes and sharp teeth. One of the admiring men in the mill where the boys carried the salmon offered them two dollars for it. Lorry would not have sold his share for ten, but Crow, as much as he loved fish, succumbed to the lure of so much money.

Another day Lorry was standing in deep, swift water, fishing in a round hole just under the Licking Dam, a famous place for catfish, though but few were caught there. All at once Lorry thought he was snagged on the bottom. Carefully he pulled and labored to free his hook. Then suddenly he made the discovery that his pole was bending down. A slow, heavy fish was pulling it. Lorry jerked with all his might. The fish retaliated with a ponderous rush, and Lorry began to slide down the slippery incline toward the deep hole. This day he was not using a reel and so could not give the fish line. It pulled him in. Lorry yelled for help, which was soon forthcoming. One fisherman took his pole and another hauled him out. Lorry had swallowed so much water that for a few moments he was incapacitated. Meanwhile the fisherman landed the fish, which was a mudcat as long as Lorry's leg and nearly a foot broad across the huge yellow and black-marked head. Lorry surely needed help to carry that fish home. He got it there alive and put it in the old tub under the hydrant, from which he was loth to take it. Tom Linden's grandfather came over to see it and offered such a price that Lorry, seeing visions of a new reel and line for Old Muddy Miser, succumbed even as had Crow.

July came, and summer with the singing locust and the hot mellow days, and low clear water at Dillon's Falls.

Lorry now went up every day except Sunday, on which day he stayed at home, being no longer compelled to attend church. Twice during this month he took Homer to Dillon's Falls, on both of which occasions singular good fortune befell the younger brother. Homer hooked more big fish that got away, and caught more small ones, and destroyed more lines and hooks, and used up more bait than any boy ever had in all the world, Lorry declared. But this experience with larger fish, coupled with Homer's success as a minnow catcher, at last made him a dyed-in-the-wool fisherman. It was settled—Homer averred he would never do anything except fish.

When August arrived Lorry persuaded his mother to win the consent of his father to permit him to camp out at Dillon's Falls. Only his mother, however, knew with whom Lorry planned to camp. Then Lorry and Homer planned that Homer was to come up to the falls occasionally, bringing a basket of supplies, and what Lorry liked more than anything—blackberry pie.

Lorry was up at dawn that first day, and, burdened with bundle, bucket and pole, he walked the three miles in record time, arriving at the pot-shop just as the sun rose.

Old Muddy Miser was eating his breakfast, which consisted of fried bass, coffee and bread.

"Here I am," Lorry announced.

"Welcome as flowers in May," replied the old fisherman. "You had a big load for a little man."

"Brought all I could carry. Bacon, lots of butter, ten pounds of sugar, and oh, a pile of stuff."

"Good! We need plenty of sugar. Will you eat a piece of fried bass?"

"You bet I will. Haven't had any breakfast. Mother got up to see me off, but I wouldn't let her bother with breakfast. I was in a hurry."

"How about your brother? Is he coming up sometimes?"

"Yes—on Friday. I made him promise not to tell the boys where he was going."

"Good! .... Now you eat some breakfast while I put this stuff away..... Aha! pie—blackberry pie! I see you have a sweet tooth, my lad. Well, it is not exactly a failing. .... What's this in the little box?"

"It's a new reel and line—for you," replied Lorry.

"For me? Well, that was kind of you, Lorry," said the old fisherman as he opened the box to take out a large silverplated, black-handled reel full of silk line. He turned it over, and around, and held it away from him, spun the handle, tried the click, and then tested the silk line.

"Rank poison, Lorry, rank poison!" he declared.

"How's fishing?" queried Lorry, with his mouth full of fried bass.

"A shade better than it has been. I've seen sign of some big ones. It's getting time for them to rant around now. Last night there was one of the biggest kind of bass feeding out at the head of the falls. He thumped the water and made furrows in that shallow rift. But he didn't work far from deep water. He's a wise old fish. Black as coal! I saw him once. I could have got a bait to him easy, but I wanted to wait for you. He'll feed there tonight."

"I'd rather see you catch a whopper first—so I'll know how to handle one when I do hook him. .... I bought you a couple dozen of those big white steel hooks you liked. The ones with the offset and short shank."

"Pray, young sir, what did you buy for yourself?" demanded the old man.

"Two new lines, some tiny minnow hooks, black and rough, the straight dull ones you like, as well as needle hooks, and a couple spools of floss silk, and a piece of beeswax."

"Wisdom, my son, wisdom. I hope when you get rich you will always show such sense. But it's only fair for me to say that I have a weakness for fishing tackle. I fear I would be extravagant."

"I *know* I will be," said Lorry, with a tone which implied as well the fact that some day he would have the money.

"Two meals a day—a hearty one for supper—are enough for fishermen," remarked the old man. "We'll have breakfast early, and supper about four. That will give us the sunset and twilight hours for fishing— which are the best, my lad. . . . . Now to wash and scour things. We must fetch a bundle of hay from the farmer's field for our bed. Then to make a box to keep minnows. Then to fix up tackle. I have located some fine mustard-seed reeds for minnow poles. We will cut some, trim them, and hang them to dry. There's plenty of work, Lorry. But you must learn there are two kinds of fishermen. Those who idle and those who work. We belong to the latter class. A rolling stone gathers no moss. A drone carries no honey to the hive. . . . . Another task today, Lorry. We must fashion a good fish knife out of an old file I have. The farmer has a grindstone in his shed. We will grind this file, and then draw the temper to make it soft. The makers of Damascus steel surely were expert in tempering."

Thus the day began and the hours flew by. While engaged at their tasks the old fisherman talked as one whose lips had long been sealed. In Lorry he had an eager listener, a worshipper whose glad eyes must have been inspiring. Every now and then he would amaze Lorry.

He would be silent and thoughtful for a while, then he would push back his battered slouch hat and halting in his task glare fixedly at Lorry. "The Hindus now—they're a wonderful race. They have habits queer to us so-called cultured people. Friendship is good. A congenial comrade helps develop the mind. But, lad, never forget that the great men have been thinkers and are not gregarious. You must begin at once to form a habit of being alone, if only for a little while every day. Go off by yourself. Sit by the falls, or in the woods, or fields. Look around you and think of what you see. Nature is all around. Make it a part of you. . . . Watch the sun set and twilight fall and the stars brighten. Thoughts will come to you."

At another time he suddenly halted in a task to ask Lorry: "Did you ever see the effect whiskey has upon a raw egg?"

"No, indeed," replied Lorry.

"Well, if you break an egg into a plate and pour whiskey over it the albumen is coagulated. In fact, the egg is cooked and turns blue. . . . . Fine stuff whiskey to take into your stomach!"

"Why do men drink?" wondered Lorry. "Is it the taste?"

"No. Not one in a thousand men really knows why he drinks. Some day you will understand."

Not until nearly four o'clock did Lorry have a little respite from his pleasant labors. He was sitting on the ledge of rock that jutted out from the pot-shop. It was a shady, beautiful spot. The green water swirled and eddied in the pool under him. Lorry shut his eyes and listened to the murmur and babble and low melodious music of the falls. There seemed no more wonderful sound than that of running water. He thought about what made it and how the water passed on, never to return again. He loved the quiet and solitude of this place, the swift, clear water with its golden gleams, and its finny denizens, the warmth of the sun and the cool of the shade, the fluttering leaves and the singing birds, the vague sense of their harmony with the infinite and the mystery of himself. A marvelous secret seemed suddenly to be revealed to Lorry, but he could not define it in lucid thoughts. It seemed, however, to have to do with his feeling of youth and the endless rapture of the years to come. The thing was here, all around him, in the swift stream, in the fragrant drowsy air, in the whispering leaves, in the creatures that swam and flew, and in himself.

Then from the pot-shop rang the old fisherman's call! "Come to the festal board!"

Lorry went in to find a supper that fully deserved such ceremonious summons. He ate until he had scarce room for the generous piece of blackberry pie. And then, after washing the pans and utensils, and storing all carefully away, he and the old fisherman took poles and bucket containing a few choice chubs and waded out to the head of the falls.

Dillon's Falls was a fascinating place to fish. The deep water ran abruptly to the notched and channeled ledge of rocks. Some of these channels were wide and had shelving sides, and led out into shoal swift water where the minnows sported. The current was just swift enough to carry a bait without letting it sink to the bottom. Lorry fished breathlessly, and watched the old fisherman. The sun sank; the hot air cooled; the rosy and gold lights changed and darkened; the bird songs gave place to chirp of insects; twilight and dusk fell, softly and magically; shadows gathered up the stream.

Neither Lorry nor Old Muddy Miser had a strike that evening. It appeared the bass were not feeding. But Lorry was full of content. Soon he lay down on the bed of hay in the loft of the pot-shop beside the old fisherman. Lorry was tired with the long day and so sleepy he scarce could keep awake. How satisfying his state! The low dreamy sound of

running water permeated the air. Mice scampered over the floor of the loft. A whippoorwill sang his lonely sweet song. The smell of new mown hay, thick and sweet in Lorry's nostrils, was the last sensation he knew before slumber claimed him.

Lorry was awakened by the singing of meadow-larks. Through the open door he saw the rays of the sun gleaming like silver fire on the mist. He smelled wood smoke, and then heard Muddy Miser below chopping wood. Lorry rolled out of his bed of hay; and the fun of it was he did not have the bother of dressing, for he had slept in shirt and trousers. With towel and soap he made for the river, shouting a merry good-morning to the old fisherman.

"Up with the lark, Lorry!" was the reply. "The early bird catches the worm."

That day passed like a swift dream, full of happy tasks, always accompanied by the low roar of the fall. At sunset, when Lorry was standing on the little hill above the pot-shop, facing the west, the old fisherman called him: "Hey, Lorry, where are you? Come a-running!"

Lorry dashed down to join the old fisherman who stood just outside of the spread of the sycamore.

"Look up there, Lorry," he said, pointing toward the head of the falls.

Lorry heard a cracking thump of a powerful fish in the water. Then he saw a white splash close of the ledge of rock, where the deep stream ran into the wide channel. An angry swirl of the water followed, then the frantic leaping of minnows, and again the cracking thump. Lorry caught a glimpse of a flashing black fish shape.

"There he is, Lorry. Ranting round after bait. We're going to hook him tonight. Fetch my pole. And hurry."

When Lorry ran down to the low place where they always waded in, Muddy Miser was taking the rocks off the minnow-box. Several large lively chubs were put into the bucket. Then they hurried out toward the head of the falls. As they neared it, the old fisherman halted Lorry and put the largest chub on the hook.

"Wade slow and easy now," admonished Old Muddy Miser.

Cautiously they waded out to a point above where the bass had been feeding.

"I saw him make a swirl just by that notch in the rock," whispered the old fisherman. "Now watch. This is business, sure."

Lorry was all eyes and tingling nerves. How intensely he felt the quiet and beauty of the place, the gleaming water mirroring the sunset clouds! He stood just back of the old fisherman who cast his bait upstream and let it float down along the ledge. It passed where they stood and floated on toward the notch. But it never reached there.

CHAPTER IX[1]

Lorry's quick eye caught a bulge of the water. The limp line halted, grew stiff, and then cut the water.

"Business!" whispered Old Muddy Miser.

The line swept steadily and slowly for a few yards and stopped just at a point opposite the apex of the notch. The old fisherman was bending forward with long pole outstretched, reaching as far as possible. Lorry saw the slight twitching of the line, and he knew the bass had not let go of the chub. How tensely and patiently the old fisherman waited! Lorry felt that he could never have done so. Then the line began to glide back up

---

[1]This chapter combines IX with part of the original X, so *The Fisherman* is reduced to ten chapters from the original eleven installments.

stream, and as it did so Muddy Miser elevated his pole and slowly followed the movement until he had to bend and reach as before, only now in the opposite direction. The bass was making for deep water. The fisherman jerked hard with forward and upward motion. The heavy bamboo pole bent double. The line hissed. Out of a sounding splash an enormous black bass leaped, mouth wide, fins bristling, body curved with fury. Down he went to swish to one side and then the other.

"Give him line!" yelled Lorry irresistibly. "You'll break him off!"

But the old fisherman never gave an inch as far as Lorry could see. He held hard on the pole and shut down on the reel with his thumb. How that pole bent and wagged! The bass came out on a stiff line, high into the air, wrestling, with a loud noise. Down he thumped to break out viciously again. Then here and there he rushed on the surface, beating the water white, making waves and swirls. He made one more leap, slower, showing his gaping gills, then he sounded, and plunged to and fro as far as the line would permit. The old fisherman began to wade back along the ledge, leading the bass toward the place where the water shoaled upon the rock. Still the pole was bent almost double. With one final desperate surge, the bass came up. Then the old fisherman drew him out of the channel into quiet water on the ledge, and farther on until the depth was no longer enough for him to swim upright. Soon he was on his side, a great, golden-black, shield-shaped fish, gasping and floundering.

"Catch him through the gills," called Old Muddy Miser. "Get a good hold before you lift!"

Lorry, in his earnest efforts, overturned the bucket and lost the bait, but he made a good job of securing the bass.

"Six pounds! One of the biggest kind!" declared the old fisherman.

"What—a—fish!" gasped Lorry. "But you never gave him an inch!"

"Lad, when you've hooked and lost as many big bass as I have, you'll be businesslike," replied Old Muddy Miser. "And even so—most of them get away."

Lorry procured a stout cord, which he ran through the mouth and gills of the bass, and then tied it securely to a willow in water deep enough for the fish to swim. Lorry watched it until dusk fell so thickly that he could no longer see. And next morning, the first thing, Lorry went down to look at the bass. It made a surge and roar in the water, splashing all over Lorry, and roused such a commotion that he gave up trying to see it until after breakfast. Then he adopted other tactics and slipped through the willows until he could peep down upon the fish. Lorry did not believe his eyes. Not only was the bass bigger than he remembered, it had changed color. From glossy bronze black with gleams of gold it had turned to greenish yellow with curved dark bars and streaks. Its eyes were black with tints of red. The wide pectoral fins moved like fans; slowly the gills opened and closed. Lorry watched it with rapt adoring eyes until Old Muddy Miser approached, knife in hand, to kill and dress it. Lorry could not remain to see the necessary task. He wanted both to keep the bass alive, and to let it go.

At night, the old fisherman set what he called trotlines, baited with live chubs, for catfish. He found a ready sale among the farmers for these fish. These lines were laid across the river in deep places with rock bottoms some distance above the falls. Usually Muddy Miser baited them before sunset and raised them next morning. But owing to the fact that he believed catfish hooked themselves early and tore out before morning he decided to raise the lines about midnight. And that night as he was getting up, he awakened Lorry.

"Come with me," said the old fisherman. "But put on your coat. It'll be chilly."

Soon Lorry found himself padding barefoot over the clay trail along the river bank between the drooping, rustling cornstalks and the moon-blanched sycamore trees, white barked and broad leaved. How weird the night! Gradually the low roar of the falls died away. Only a faint hum of insects broke the lonely solitude. Presently Old Muddy Miser led the way under the dark trees, down the steep bank to a little flat-boat moored to some roots.

"Get in the back and sit trim," said the old fisherman. "This vessel was not built for two."

Lorry observed that when Old Muddy Miser seated himself in the front end, the boat settled alarmingly in the water, until only a few inches of gunwale stood above the surface. The old man extended his arm down and grasped the trot-line, which had been made fast to a root. He lifted it out of the water across his knees, and by pulling on it caused the little flat-boat to glide out into the stream.

"Business!" exclaimed the old fisherman. "We've got one. He's heavy, too."

Lorry saw the jerking of the trot-line and heard it cut the water. What fun this was! Everybody in the world was asleep while he and the old fisherman were out at midnight, in the lonely solitude, hauling on a big catfish. Lorry gazed about him, up and down the pale, duskily gleaming river, full of shadows from the lofty trees. The moon was in its last quarter, misshapen, dull orange in hue and strange. A water-fowl croaked from the reedy bank; tiny waves lapped against the boat.

Gradually Old Muddy Miser drew the boat toward the middle of the stream until he was close to the fish. More slowly he moved and finally came right above the struggling quarry. Then it appeared to be give-and-take for a little. But at last the fish seemed to be coming up.

Suddenly there was a tremendous splashing and flopping. Water splashed in Lorry's face. He felt cold water on his feet. Gazing down he found the little boat half full of water.

"Mr. Miser, we've sprung a leak," announced Lorry. "We're sinking."

The old fisherman looked back over his shoulder, and still held to the trot-line.

"Well, so we are," he replied, and dropped the trot-line, which twanged on the water. "Paddle fast, lad, or we'll have to swim."

Lorry picked up the paddle and began desperately to gain the closer shore. But he could not make much headway. Slowly the water came up and filled the boat. Gradually it settled, letting them down, legs and hips, and waists, until at last they were up to their necks.

"Swim for it, Lorry," said the old fisherman, as he struck out.

He lost his hat, which Lorry secured and put on his own head. Lorry saw the old man's shaggy locks bobbing in front of him. Thus they swam into the deep shadow cast by the trees and on into the gloom to where they could touch bottom and wade out.

"Lad, we lost a big mudcat, and we have a job of building another boat," said the old fisherman. "See here, your eyes are sharp. Lead the way up this bank. . . . That water was cold."

Lorry led the way up the brushy bank, through the belt of timber, and down along the fields to the head of the falls.

"It's bad crossing here at night," said Old Muddy Miser. "But it's a long walk down to the bridge and then up."

"I can find the safe places," vouchsafed Lorry. "Get a good stout stick to lean on and follow me."

Lorry knew every rock and ledge and channel and rift on the falls. He had confidence that he could cross here at the most dangerous place in pitch darkness. So he waded in, getting his bearings from the black clump of sycamores on the other side of the river, from the white places and dark channels, from the feel of water and rock; and so, by devious turns and careful wading, he led the old man across without mishap.

"Well done, Lorry," declared the old fisherman. "Now let's get out of these wet clothes and into dry ones."

Homer's day arrived and Lorry started early to meet him, crossing the covered bridge, and getting almost to the stone culvert before he espied his brother swinging along with a basket in each hand.

Homer was perspiring freely, and the freckles stood out markedly in his pale face.

"I was lookin' for you," he said as Lorry took the baskets, and his next words were a query as to the fishing. Lorry found him immensely curious to hear about Old Muddy Miser. By the time they reached the pot-shop, Homer had been regaled with so much history of the past few days' fishing and the possibilities of today, that he was bewildered.

"Well, glad to see you, boy," was the old fisherman's hearty greeting. "You don't favor Lorry in looks. But anyone would know you were brothers. . . . Now, boys, amuse yourselves. I've this boat to work on so I can't wade around with you. . . . And, Lorry, here's news I've been keeping from you. There's the biggest kind of a bass in Sycamore Hole, under that log."

"No! When'd you see him?" asked Lorry eagerly.

"Yesterday. I dropped a big shiner in that dark hole under the log. He came swooping up for it, a big yellow bass over five pounds, and after he took the bait he flapped his tail out of the water. I missed him clean. Then I decided to leave him alone. Now you can get a bite out of him. But wait till at least four o'clock this afternoon. Keep back out of sight and make a long cast. Remember your weakness. Don't hit him too soon."

Homer was thirteen years old now, and had long grown out of his plumpness to a slender stripling, lithe and strong.

"Homer, I've got a program for today," announced Lorry. "First I'll have fun seeing you slip around and bust yourself wading on the falls, trying to catch minnows. Then we'll go up to Bartlett's Run. Just wait till you see some of the holes up there! Then we'll come back and fish some places where I know you'll get bites. There's a pretty good sized mudcat I'd like to hook you on to. I know where there's bunch of goggle-eyes. They'll bite on little minnows and it's great to catch them. After that we'll have supper. Mr. Miser can cook corn and bass. Oh, my! Then we'll go down to Sycamore Hole after that big bass."

"Great!" said Homer. "But I promised Mother I'd be back by dark. I've got to keep my word, so's I can come up again."

"Don't worry. Mr. Burgess, the farmer, always drives to town late on Fridays. He stays all night in town so he can be at market early Saturday. He said you could ride home with him."

"By golly!" exclaimed Homer, in ecstasy.

The day of sport began and the gods of nature were propitious. Great white clouds sailed the azure sky; the golden sunlight streamed down at intervals; then shadows rode across the waters and hills. Never had Lorry seen the falls so alive with hungry chubs. Homer did everything Lorry expected and more besides. He slipped all over and sat down often. He flung chubs far across the water, and missed ten for every one he hooked. He broke the thin silk line, and at last the slender reed pole. The fascination of this fishing for game little chubs took hold of him; the difficulties he determined to master. But it took time and study, and Homer was over-anxious. Still he caught a few chubs. The climax of fun for Lorry came when he maneuvered to have Homer step carelessly on a particularly innocent-looking incline of rock. This clean slanting rock was a delusion, as Lorry had found to his cost. As luck would have it, just as Homer hooked a huge chub, he stepped on the treacherous incline. His feet flew up and he alighted squarely on his back to slide like a streak down into deep water. His red head bobbed up, his hat went floating on the current. Yet even in such straits he thought of Lorry's pole and was careful not to break it. Lorry pulled him out and rescued his hat. Then he had his great laugh.

"Gee! That rock came up and hit me!" exclaimed Homer, not in the least suspicious.

At Bartlett's Run, Homer acquitted himself nobly, walking fearlessly across the slender log that spanned the stream, leaping from bank to bank in Lorry's footsteps, and catching more fine minnows in a short space of time than he ever had before. Homer did not talk very much, but it was plain to Lorry that he was charmed with Bartlett's Run. Indeed, for Lorry, something new was added to this wild creek in guiding his brother there. Meadowlarks and blackbirds sang continuously. It was a glorious summer day, with hot sunshine, cool shade, a fragrant breeze off the fields, and utter solitude. Lorry was loth to break away from it all. Back they strode down the shady trail under sycamores and beside the rustling corn, across the murmuring river to the pot-shop.

Not without misgivings and reluctance did Lorry lend his fishing pole to Homer. But he calculated it would be much better for his brother to break his pole than Old Muddy Miser's. Lorry took the old man's pole, and gave Homer his without a word of caution. He knew Homer would be too worried about the pole to enjoy the fishing. Therefore, Lorry swallowed his dread and trusted to luck.

Assuredly fisherman's luck fell to Homer Dunn that day. Not a hole or a channel but held a biting bass! Homer hooked so many that his losses were dwarfed by excitement. He had no time to dwell on one which leaped to throw the hook, or another that tore loose in its first fierce rush. Several heavy bass took Homer's bait and never showed themselves, so that when they broke away he was no wiser.

In the deep black eddy where foam globules floated round and round,

Homer caught ten big goggle-eyes. These voracious fish were easy to hook. Homer could not miss them. And every time he jerked one out, he squealed with delight.

They did not get half way down the falls. And lastly Lorry introduced Homer to a friendly catfish that he hooked himself. This was in a still dark pocket of water under the west bank of rock, and when a bait was dropped into it, no doubt it fell right on the nose of the mudcat. Homer hooked it, and the fish came out with a plunge into the shallow water. Lorry saw it plainly, a speckled dark-colored mudcat fully five pounds in weight. Homer had never felt so heavy a fish nor seen such capers. He got the line tangled round the reel handle so that it would no longer pay out.

"Run after him!" yelled Lorry.

Now Homer was the fleetest runner of all the boys in Hainesville. It did not matter to him what the bottom was like. He ran. He ploughed up the water. He tried to catch up with the darting catfish, and was working valiantly when he lost his balance and began to fall. He went down, face foremost, pole extended with both hands, and he went clear under. When he floundered up the mudcat had broken the line. Wringing wet, covered with slime, bewildered and chagrined, he presented a most ludicrous figure.

"Lorry—did—you—see him?" he panted, wildly.

"You bet—I did," replied Lorry, trying to smother his laughter. "Nice mudcat. You let him overrun your reel, and the line tangled. Too bad."

"He was—long—as my leg," replied Homer, mournfully. "And he broke—your line. Will he die, with that hook stickin' in him?"

"No. That old catfish will be back in this hole tonight. And sometime we'll get him again."

They returned to the pot-shot and wrung the water out of Homer's shirt and trousers.

"Come to the festal board!" called the old fisherman from below. And as much as Lorry enjoyed that sumptuous supper, he enjoyed more seeing his brother eat. Next to that he had delight in relating to Old Muddy Miser the history of Homer's exploits that day.

"Better turn your line around and try the fresh end on that big bass in Sycamore Hole," was the old fisherman's advice.

Lorry was careful to do this, and to rig his sinker and hook with particular care, not unmindful of Homer's studious observance.

"Don't hit at that bass too quick!" was Muddy Miser's parting injunction.

"I won't. If he takes my bait, I'll wait as long as I can stand it," called back Lorry with a doubtful laugh.

To save time and unnecessary wading, Lorry took the path along the bank downstream to a point opposite Sycamore Hole. Once down over the rugged rocky ledge the rest of the way was easy wading. But to make sure there would be no mishap Lorry carried pole and bucket himself, and went slowly. At last he halted thirty feet from Sycamore Hole on a bare flat of ridged rock, upon which he set the bucket.

"Here's the place, Homer," said Lorry pointing, "and there's the sunken log under which the big bass hides. I've caught some nice ones here, but never a big one."

"Gee!" was all Homer said. His brown flashing eyes, however, were expressive enough as they roved over the foamy deep hole, and the dark green depths of shadow under the old log. All about this irregular shaped basin were ruts and rifts, channels and chasms, melodious with low murmur of swift water.

Lorry knelt beside the bucket with his pole over his knees and the hook in his hand.

"There's a big blue-fin shiner in here," he said, scooping up a double handful of minnows. "I'm going to try it first." The bait in question was not easy to catch, but at length Lorry secured it and gently slipped the hook through its lips. Then he dropped the bait in the water at his feet and stood up.

"Come on—right close to me," he said breathlessly to Homer. And as if stalking game in the woods, he slipped closer to the edge of the pool. "Keep your eyes peeled, Homer. I'm going to cast just this side of the log."

For his life Lorry could not have subdued the trembling of his body nor the rapid beats of his heart. Because of this over-excitement he was likely to make a mess of his cast. Nevertheless he strove with all his might to do what he knew would be right. He let out all the line he could manage, some few feet more than the length of his pole, and then swinging the frantically wiggling shiner easily to the left as far as the line would go, he made a long sweep out over the pool and cast the bait very close to where he had calculated. Scarcely had the shiner splashed on the surface when out of the depths loomed a shadowy shape. It came swiftly up. It flashed yellow, and acquired the graceful outline of a big bass, instinct with life and ferocity. In one quick snap it took the shiner. Lorry's keen eyes saw the tiny white floating scales that told the story of that tragedy. Lazily the bass turned. His broad tail came out, flapped on the surface. Then the yellow fish shape glided back to disappear in the dark lair.

"Oh-h!" gasped Homer.

Lorry tingled all over. He let his line pay out until it stopped. Then the little vibrations told him what was going on. He must wait—wait—wait! But it seemed his very veins were bursting. Already he had waited ages. It was not with his consent that he jerked. The act was involuntary. Up shot line and hook, to whistle in the air. Lorry had missed hooking the bass.

"Too soon!" he cried, poignantly. "I was afraid of that. . . . Homer, a big bass must have *time*!—but I never scratched him. He'll take another bait."

Homer appeared to recover his power of speech, but what he said was so incoherent that Lorry could not understand him. Then with trembling eager fingers Lorry put on another bait, this time the biggest chub in the bucket. Sight of it silenced Homer's ravings. Then Lorry drew a deep breath. The chances were in his favor that the bass would take at least another minnow. With this heavier bait Lorry made a better cast. The chub splashed on the surface and swam under. It was met by a yellow flash. Smash! The water boiled white where the bass broke. Lorry did not see what had become of the chub, but he knew anyway. The bass was gone this time as quickly as it had appeared. Lorry's line swept down and down—then stopped. Lorry waited. The sweat came out all over him, so great was his desire to jerk and his determination not to until the right time. His intensity of feeling grew with the gentle vibrations of his line. At last he swept up the pole hard, but not hard enough to break the line. Lorry was learning restraint. His pole bent double by a sudden irresistible pull.

"I've got him, Homer!" yelled Lorry at the top of his lungs.

Then began a battle that for excitement and action beat any that had ever befallen Lorry. The bass did not leap. He surged about the pool, running under the shelving edges, but Lorry, keen to frustrate such moves ran close to the edges to hold his pole out so that his line would not cut on any sharp rock. To and fro, up and down this pool the bass dashed. Lorry ran with him, so he did not have to pay out line. Suddenly the fish shot up one of the channels. It was wide and deep at the mouth, but it narrowed. The bass swam on; Lorry held hard. How his pole wagged! Homer was yelling. Lorry feared the line would break and he had to yield. The bass swam on up the channel to where it was scarcely a foot wide. He was going to work on up and out into the long hole above. Lorry knew this would spell calamity. Suddenly he had an inspiration.

"Homer, head him off! Run up and jump in the run. Stop him!"

Heedless of slippery rocks Homer flew splashingly to a point above Lorry's line, and plumped down into the run. The water came above his knees. He kicked and beat at a great rate. Suddenly he screamed. "He bumped into me! He couldn't get by!"

So indeed it proved. The bass turned back to Sycamore Hole, and after a few desperate surges he slowed up. Then Lorry put more strain on him,

and gradually achieving something of calmness, he tried to handle the bass after the manner of the old fisherman. To his utter amaze and rapture the battle appeared to be in his favor. The bass came up, wallowed and splashed. He was beaten. Lorry, quick to recognize this, dragged the fish out of the deep hole into a channel, and from that into a shallow place.

"Here, Homer, hold my pole,"[2] shouted Lorry, and the instant he got it into Homer's shaking hands he pounced upon the exhausted bass and secured it through the gills. "Oh, look—look at him."

"I'm lookin'," shouted Homer rapturously.

That was a tremendous moment for Lorry. His first big bass! And was it not wonderful to have Homer see him catch it? Long they gazed at the prize and much they exclaimed. Then they hurried back to the pot-shop, forgetting to bring the bucket. Lorry was so eager to exhibit his catch that he let Homer carry his pole, and did not see that he carried it tip first, an unpardonable sin for a fisherman.

"Good!" exclaimed Old Muddy Miser. "Five pounds. Maybe a shade less. But we'll call it five. Now, lad, I'm just as glad as I can be. You must send the bass home to your folks."

"But I want to keep him!" cried Lorry.

"Pooh! You'll catch more and bigger ones," rejoined Old Muddy Miser.

"Oh, Lorry, please let me take him," begged Homer. "It'll please father, and he won't kick on me comin' up next week."

This cost Lorry a terrible wrench, but he suffered the old fisherman to kill the bass and watched him dress it. Soon then Homer was sitting on the front seat of the farm wagon with Mr. Burgess. As they drove away Lorry waved his hand.

"Next Friday!" called back Homer, happily.

CHAPTER X

The old pot-shop with its broken pottery and dry musty loft, and open clay-floored room, always redolent of wood smoke, came to be home for Lorry. Seldom did anyone except the farmer and his hired hand pass by the head of the falls. The country road and the railroad lay far to the other side, beyond the wide cornfield. The boys who came to Dillon's Falls to

---

[2]This passing of a rod to an accomplice before the fish is landed is not condoned by either modern angling ethics or the rules for records of the International Game Fish Association. However, this story was written 15 years before the IGFA was founded, and it describes a scene that occurred more than 35 years before that. I think we can forgive the boys for doing what came naturally!

fish never ventured near Old Muddy Miser. Fear of him had been in-grained in them long before their fishing activities. Lorry used to marvel how he, too, had once been frightened of the very name of the old hermit. But how ridiculous for anyone to fear him! It was all a mistake. Lorry began to ponder the question of whether or not the stigma of ruined life and wrecked career was not also all a mistake. Old Muddy Miser was good, not bad. The few country children thereabouts did not flee at sight of him. Rather they ran to him. The poor farmers profited by fish to eat as often when they could not pay as when they could. This old man was not mean. He loved the fish and birds and flowers and bees and all the divine inhabitants of that environment. He was a treasure trove of valuable knowledge, and he had a gift of talk. The days sped by swift as the flight of larks and it seemed to Lorry that each day left him incalculably richer, older, different.

The lofty cornstalks changed from green to yellow; the golden rod now fringed every path along the streams; brown-eyed daisies peeped from the grass and sedge. August and the harvest moon was time for bass of the biggest kind. One evening between sundown and dark Lorry caught three at his favorite place at the head of the falls. They weighed four, four and a quarter, and four and a half pounds. All taken in one hour! Lorry could not quite believe the marvelous happening. But he knew that he was growing into a fisherman.

The day came for the long-talked-of camping trip to the mouth of Poverty Run. The name alone had magic power to entrance Lorry. What boy had ever fished the marvelous holes in that vicinity? They packed buckets, baskets, blankets, poles; and Lorry was not likely to forget the six-mile walk.

Poverty Run was wilder than Bartlett's, more beautiful than Joe's Run, and a paradise for little fish. The first time Lorry tried it, he jerked minnows out as fast as he could swing the pole; and every now and then he would hook something heavy that broke the silk line. How well, indeed, that he had plenty of line and abundance of little hooks!

Licking Creek was narrower up here and had stretches of swift water running into deep holes under shelving clay banks. Like the old fisher-man, Lorry favored a place where he could wade in from the shallow side and cast a bait into the coveted waters. Before dark they had caught all the bass they could carry. Lorry's largest was two pounds, but Old Muddy Miser had one close to six.

"I'll clean them tonight and pack them down tomorrow," said the old fisherman. "We must sell what we can't eat."[1]

---

[1]Times change and so do cultural perspectives. During the 1920s, the largemouth and small-

They had pitched their camp on a small island of sand and gravel at the upper end of which was a huge pile of driftwood and a clump of willows. The green foliage was to provide shelter. Lorry was tremendously alive to the wilderness of the spot. The stream ran swiftly in front of their camp, down to a wide expanse of smooth water that Old Muddy Miser declared was the best bass ground he had ever fished. The night was cool, making the campfire most welcome. Herons and ducks swished by in the darkness overhead, uttering mysterious cries. Soon Lorry was in bed, snug under the blanket. To be sure the bed was hard sand, but that was of no moment to him. He was so sleepy that his eyelids kept closing, yet he hated to succumb. The rush of water, the chirp of crickets, the call of whippoorwill seemed here infinitely wilder and more lonely. The dark sharp foliage of the willows waved to and fro between him and the star-studded sky. The last he remembered was the flickering of the campfire.

Sometime during the night he awoke. The hour must have been late. Gray mist obscured everything. Out of it came the low rush and babble and gurgle of the running stream. There was no other sound. How weird and wild this lonely island! Yet it did not seem wholly unfamiliar to Lorry. He felt that his thought of it was like a dream of something vague, long past, yet true.

Next day Lorry was left to his own devices while the old fisherman undertook the long walk to sell his fish. There and back was twelve miles. Lorry spent the morning on Poverty Run, going upstream quite far to where it had high grassy banks, rills and pools. He saved all the choicest bait, and then out of sheer pleasure in his skill and the sport of it he caught minnows by the score, to let them go.

During the early part of the afternoon he stayed in camp watching for the return of his comrade. But Old Muddy Miser did not come, and at last the call of the bass was too great for Lorry. He went upstream to the holes fished the night before and caught a string of bass that now he called small. Not long since would he have considered them huge! Again he returned to camp. The old fisherman was not in sight. The sun was getting low, the shadows were lengthening, the heat of the day declining. Lorry took his bucket of bait and his pole and hurried down to the great pool so wonderfully spoken of by Old Muddy Miser.

At the foot of the island there was a shallow flat, rock-bottomed, that led to the left shore. Here bass were feeding. Lorry saw swirls and splashes, jumping minnows, and furrows on the surface. Then he heard

mouth bass were made gamefishes in most states, hence, illegal to sell. Remember, however, that ZG is describing conditions in the 1880s.

as solid a thump as could have been made by a cow kicking off flies, as she stood knee deep in the water. "Whew! Could that be a bass?" asked Lorry, as he gazed around.

The sound had, indeed, been made by a bass. No other fish could have started the circling waves from the center of that pool. Lorry saw the yellow shadow of a flat rock, and decided this was where the big bass lived. Never had Lorry waded so cautiously and noiselessly. Bass were feeding all around him, but it was the big one, far out, that he wanted to reach. Lorry waded up to his hips, as far as he could go. Then he cast for the marked spot.

There came a roaring splash. The bass hit the bait so hard that he nearly jerked the pole out of Lorry's hands. Also he felt the hook and leaped, a magnificent fish, larger than the six-pounder Old Muddy Miser had caught. Lorry was paralyzed. It had happened too swiftly. He expected to see his bait and hook go flying. The bass did throw the bait, but he had caught the hook. Down he cracked and plunged away! Then Lorry, coming to his senses, set the hook deep. The bass made a churning, furious splash, then swept like lightning downstream. Lorry's reel whizzed. All the line passed out. Then he ran pellmell through the water, pole extended, ploughing like a horse. Getting to where it was shallow he made better time. But the bass gained the swift water below. He pulled so hard that he overbalanced Lorry. Head first he fell, ramming the precious pole into the rocks. When Lorry floundered up, the pole was broken, his line was limp. The monster bass had escaped. Lorry wound in his line, to find that the hook had straightened out.

"O! What—a—bass!" choked Lorry, absolutely heart-broken. "Oh, now I know—what Mr. Miser meant!"

Terrible as seemed that moment, it yet held something familiar—the same old pang of loss. It had grown with the years. Lorry stared at the deep swift stretch where his largest bass had vanished. How impossible to bring him back! It was as if there was no hope anywhere. At last, disconsolate, Lorry returned to camp. Old Muddy Miser was there, busy around the campfire. Sympathetically he listened to Lorry's tale of woe and carefully examined the rod.

"Lad, nothing is ever as bad as it seems," he said. "I can mend this pole—make it as good as ever. You didn't leave a hook in that old buster. He lives in that hole. *And we'll catch him!*"

Three evenings after that, Lorry was to see the old fisherman hook the same bass, stop his runs and turn him around.

"Take my pole!" yelled the old fisherman forcing it into Lorry's hands. Indeed Lorry could not have resisted had he tried. And there was a grand fight left in that bass. He leaped only once, but this was four feet into the air, so close to Lorry that he splashed water all over him. Only Lorry knew the weakness of his legs! If the bass had known enough to dash away again he would have pulled Lorry off his feet. But wearily he wove to and fro. The hook was deep. Soon Old Muddy Miser lifted the old scarred bronze-backed warrior out on the sand.

"One of the biggest kind, Lorry. . . . Seven pounds!"

"Let's keep him alive—as long as we can," replied Lorry, overcome by the sight of that bass.

September found them back at Dillon's Falls with the day near at hand when Lorry must go home. The farmer brought news that Dr. Dunn was trying to sell his property. This surprised Lorry and shocked him into memory. It was then he confessed to his friend the trouble and disgrace he had brought upon his people.[2]

"It is good, if you never do it again," replied the old man.

"My God! . . . I would die first," declared Lorry, moved to passion.

"Lad, we have had a wonderful happy time together. I wish I might have had a son like you. . . . We have talked. I have told you much. I could not ask more in response than you have given. But I never yet gave you an ideal of womanhood. Perhaps I couldn't find the right words. And so, I'll only tell you two things. Never forget them. When you think of women, think of them as you do of your mother. All women are mothers of all men. . . . And never in your life lay a hand on any woman unless you honestly love her."

Lorry did not make promises lightly. But he made this one ringingly, despite the fact that he only vaguely understood and was troubled by a strange emotion.

Old Muddy Miser walked as far as the covered bridge with Lorry. It was plain he was going to be lonely. At last he halted and shook Lorry's hand. The sun had set and dusk lay in the hollows of the hills. The water below the falls roared low and sadly.

"I—I won't say goodbye," said Lorry, and hurried into the shadowy tunnel of the bridge, rattling the loose boards with his bare feet. He did not look back. It would not have been any use, for his eyes were blinded by tears.

---

[2]It was not Lorry, alias Pearl Gray, who brought disgrace to the Dunn, alias Gray, family. It was the father, Dr. Gray, who in 1890 made a reckless investment of all the family's savings and lost everything. He went to Washington, D.C., to see whether his Senator or Representative could be of any use in recovering the money, and when the trip was unsuccessful, Dr. Gray didn't have the courage to return to Zanesville where everyone knew of his disaster. He arranged for his wife to move the family to Columbus, Ohio, where Dr. Gray went to establish a new dental practice and a fresh reputation.

"SEA ANGLING"

Introduction

This is an old story—the story of a man from the interior of a continent who, long after his childhood, first sees the ocean and is overawed by its majesty and mystery. Zane Grey turned to the romantic poets for help in trying to comprehend the sea, and he incorporated many of their perceptions—such as breaking waves as "wild white horses"—into his own sometimes lyric prose and envied those among them who, like George Gordon, Lord Byron, had known the sea all their lives:

> "And I have loved thee, Ocean! and my joy
> Of youthful sports was on thy breast to be
> Borne, like thy bubbles, onward: from a boy
> I wanton'd with thy breakers—they to me
> Were a delight; and if the freshening sea
> Made them a terror—'twas a pleasing fear,
> For I was as it were a child of thee,
> And trusted to thy billows far and near,
> And laid my hand upon thy mane—as I do here."

One can picture Zane Grey at the fishing camp on Long Key in the Florida Keys or at his home on Catalina Island overlooking the harbor and the blue Pacific, reading Byron, Keats, and Shelley for inspiration and understanding.

The line from Byron which he quotes in the following article that first appeared in the August 1922 issue of *Outdoor America* is from the 178th stanza of the fourth canto of *Childe Harold's Pilgrimage*. The entire verse is:

This never-before-published picture shows some of Zane Grey's saltwater tackle and his fishing books. Although his sons and ZG reserved a special place in their private lives for steelhead trout fishing in Oregon, his enduring angling fame rests on his pioneering efforts in the sea.

"There is a pleasure in the pathless woods,
There is a rapture on the lonely shore,
There is society, where none intrudes,
By the deep Sea, and music in its roar:
I love not Man the less, but Nature more,
From these our interviews, in which I steal
From all I may be, or have been before,
To mingle with the Universe, and feel
What I can ne'er express, yet cannot all conceal."

GWR

SEA ANGLING

In my boyhood I was a haunter of the brooks and streams; and my first fishing tackle was a willow or mustard stick, a piece of cord and a bent pin. Pumpkin-seed sunfish, goggle-eyes, bull-heads, chubs, and shiners were the little fish of those Ohio waters of my youth. Even today the names bring a thrill, a haunting something from the days that are no more. They sound like poetry.

From these minnows I progressed to the angling for black-bass and trout; and for many years rivers and lakes and mountain-streams were a passion with me. How well I knew the rocky shores of noble inland waters! The shady shelving bank of lily-dotted lake! The swift amber-colored brooks under the hemlocks! Like Van Dyke[1] I can never see a little river without wanting to fish in it.

But of late years most of my angling energies and contemplations have been devoted to the sea. As I have written to try to make the multitude love the open and the wild, and the fast-disappearing loneliness and beauty of the southwest, so have I written to anglers of the thrill, the mystery, and the tremendousness of the sea. Whether an angler stands in the foamy surf, with the sweet salt scent of the Atlantic in his face, or canoes the shallow white shoals of the coral reefs, or trolls from a launch

---

[1] There are two Van Dykes in the pantheon of American outdoor writing. Henry was born in 1852 and published *Fisherman's Luck* in 1899 and *Out of Doors in the Holy Land* in 1908. John Charles Van Dyke was born in 1856 and spent most of his professional life teaching art history at Rutgers University, not far from where his cousin, Henry, was teaching literature at Princeton between stints as ambassador to the Netherlands and Luxembourg and service during World War I as a Navy chaplain. John Charles published *The Still-Hunter* in 1882, and the book was enlarged and re-copyrighted by his son, Theodore, the year his father died: 1932. It is Henry Van Dyke, who died in 1933, to whom ZG is referring.

Even in the oceanic paradises of Polynesia where Zane Grey caught record sailfish and the first 1,000-pound marlin, he never abandoned his first love of fishing small streams. Here he uses a fly rod to catch *nato* (a type of perch called Tahitian "trout") in the Tautira District of Tahiti in the early 1930s.

in the warm blue waters of the Gulf Stream, or scans the vast heaving glassy swells of the Pacific—it is all the same—there is a fascination and reward apart from the capture of fish.

Inland waters lull me to dreaming repose and content. The babble of a brook under a gray old cliff has a haunting music. A swift dark-green river bordered with pines is a joy. A placid forest-skirted lake, with the white camp tent gleaming on shore, is something devoutly to be wished.

But there is more to the ocean. Salmon-fishermen who have mastered the highest art of angling must never forget that salmon run up out of the sea. It is the sea that makes the silver lord of the Restigouche the incomparable fish he is. It is the sea that makes the pearl tinted steelhead of the Rogue so savage and wonderful. It is the salt water that develops the dynamic bonefish. Which is to say that the sea is the mother of all fish, and for that matter, of all life on the earth.

It may take me a long time to tell what I have learned from the sea; and I will never tell all, because I am forever learning. But the capture of fish is not all, nor the half of the secret of the spell of the sea. If I write, it must be to impress this, as well as to narrate an adventure with some denizen of the deep.

Byron sang, "there is a rapture on the lonely shore." It is true. And that rapture is a million times more to me than the fighting of a fish. Nevertheless I would not want to develop intellectually and spiritually to such a point that I would never want to pull hard on a fish. I confess to a desire to retain a little of the barbarian.

Long Key² Notes, February 13.

The day is one of those windy days when the sea is rough and a roily green, and the waves slap on the beach. There is a continuous wrestling roar in the palms, and an incessant waving of the long leaves, and a wonderful quivering of the slender blades. The shadows seem to chase over the white sand, and all around and above gleams the broad bright glare of the sun. The wind is cool and the sun is hot. For a while I lay in the hammock under the palms, in the favored place where I have been so many years. It seems always restful there, musical—conducive to dreams. No wonder few great thinkers are developed in the tropics. The sun, though a gift of life, retards intellect. Perhaps the sun is only concerned with fertility and fecundity. Yet more happiness must abide in the tropics than in any other zone.

February 18.

Days pass. Last night I wandered up and down the beach. The day had been stormy and the night was dark, with but few stars. A strong wind

---

²Despite the fact that the Florida Keys are a long way from ZG's principal homes in Pennsylvania and California, his links to Long Key only ended in 1935 when a hurricane smashed the old fishing camp with 15-foot-high walls of water. In ZG's foreword to Van Campen Heilner's *Salt Water Fishing* (1936), Grey wrote: "It is sad to think that Long Key, doomed by a hurricane, is gone forever. But the memory of that long white winding lonely shore of coral sand, and the green surf, and the blue Gulf Stream will live in memory."

blew off the sea. In the palm grove there were moaning and wailing of wind, and moving spectres of shadows and loneliness to suit even me. During the night I awoke sometime late. All was still. The storm wind had gone. I could hear the faint murmur of the reef.

This morning dawned stormy and all day the horizon was banked with rolling dark clouds and palls of rain. A stiff cool breeze whipped out of the northeast. R. C. and Lone Angler Wiborn[3] and I went fishing up on the inside, and were caught in one gusty squall of rain. It cleared off to the eastward. But at sunset there were clouds all around, a magnificent spectacle. We rode one hour facing the setting sun, and no words could adequately describe the panorama. The clouds except in the direct west were a soft misty rainy gray. In the west they were lighter. The sun began to set in a pale glow of silver. But this gradually changed, colored, growing bright, with tints of rose and gold. Just in front of the sun was a broken film of cloud, silver streaked, with fire at the lower edge. To the north a wan sun-dog shone, yellow and orange, a little blue, and white. An elusive phenomenon!

At last this sunset made up for its rather steely and cold beginning. All of a sudden the whole west lighted up—yellow—gold, with pink shades, and wonderful rounded edges of radiant silver, and coppery and bronze patches showing through the thinned parts of clouds. To the east a magnificent columnar bank stood up, dark purple, with a sunset-flushed pillar of creamy white standing above it into the blue.

The sea was rippling pale green, and did not reflect the color of the sky. The feeling I had was of the wide openness of it all, the spacious hall of the world, at the last bright steps of dying day. Pelicans sailed low along the surface of the sea, and gulls winged buoyant flight into the sunset. The lacy line of cocoanut palms bent their graceful leaves away from the wind.

March 19.

This is my last day at Long Key for this year. It is a windy day, and sunny, though not one of the white days. A steady hard trade-wind is

---

[3]R. C. is Romer Carl, Zane Grey's younger brother; and "Lone Angler" Wiborn is Dr. J. Auburn Wiborn, a dentist like ZG, who found ways to escape his practice in Santa Barbara, California, almost as often as ZG got away from his earlier office. Lone Angler earned his sobriquet by eschewing a captain or mate when angling off the California coast. He also held a reputation at the Tuna Club for frequently releasing big tuna and marlin that would have earned him buttons and prizes galore had he brought the fish ashore.

blowing from the east! The sea is moaning and the grove is roaring. Fantastic shadows of shade move over the sunlit sand under the palms. The long leaves droop and swing and curve, with their blades quivering. I wonder if what I call leaves are not really branches and the long blades of green narrow-like bayonets, are not the leaves. Both branch and leaf, perhaps![4] I wonder what Ruskin[5] would have written about these cocoanut palms. Something beautiful and unforgettable! Born for wind, yet in defiance of the hurricane!

What of the mystery of the sea? It can never be known. It is endless, infinite. An angler cannot spend so much as an hour along the beach or on the sea without being confronted by something mysterious.

> "Below the thunders of the upper deep,
> Far, far beneath in the abysmal sea,
> His ancient, dreamless, uninvaded sleep
> The Kraken sleepeth; faintest sunlights flee
> About his shadowy sides; above him swell
> Huge sponges of millennial growth and height,
> And far away into the sickly light,
> From many a wondrous grotto and secret cell.
> Unnumber'd and enormous polypi
> Winnow with giant arms the slumbering green."

Avalon, July 15.

For me the sea serpent is no myth. I believe that some day I will have a glimpse of one.[6] How many strange creatures have I seen!

What of the tremendousness of the ocean? Contending tides, the vast world-wide swell that heaves across the deep, the unnumbered leagues of water, the source of storms, the maker of rain, fog, dew—progenitors of

---

[4]Modern botanists hedge (pun intended) by calling the coconut palm's fronds *leaves* and the numerous gracefully drooping, "narrow-like bayonets," to use ZG's expression, *leaflets*.

[5]Although John Ruskin (1819–1900) is known primarily today as an English art critic and social welfare crusader, 60 years ago he was also known as a poet and essayist whose rich prose style would have appealed mightily to Zane Grey.

[6]During the 1920s, a good many Catalina Tuna Club members saw a sea serpent called the San Clemente Monster. Ralph Bandini described it as "a thick body surmounted by a reptilian head and with God awful eyes." David Starr Jordan suggested it was only an elephant seal; others thought it might be a gray whale. But then neither Jordan nor the gray whale theorists ever saw the San Clemente Monster which disappeared during World War II, allegedly the victim of U.S. anti-submarine measures.

life on the earth, the leviathans of the abysmal depths,—these are a few of the tremendous facts of the sea. Many anglers like accuracy and fact as well as the dreamful and possible. Let me chronicle as simply as I can my latest proof of some of the things I have been asserting.

Yesterday, July 14, was the date of my first sight of a broadbill swordfish for 1922. It was my third day out on the sea this season. For my brother R. C. it was his fortieth day out. He had sighted fourteen swordfish and had gotten one strike.

This first swordfish for me had a wide range between tail and dorsal fin, both of which showed above the water. This is a sure sign of a big fish.

R. C. held the rod. Capt. Sid[7] stood at the wheel. I directed operations. We used a three foot barracuda for bait, and circled the swordfish with long line out, keeping far away from him. On the fourth circle we got the bait within fifty feet of him. He turned away and went under. But we waited tense and thrilling. Presently he hit that bait so hard he nearly jerked the rod out of R. C.'s hands. We all yelled. At intervals of a moment or two he hit the bait again, four times in all. Then he took it and swam off.

R. C. let him go until several hundred feet of the line had slipped off the reel. The swordfish came up, evidently to throw the hook, and he threshed on the surface. Then R. C. reeling and pumping hard, hooked the swordfish. He went down.

The time was 9:30 in the morning. We were ten miles off Catalina Island, and a number of tuna fishermen with kites flying[8] were within sight of us. Jump,[9] the famous light tackle expert, saw us and ran down to snap some pictures of R. C. hauling on the swordfish. Later Adams and Hooper,[10] two of the old Tuna Club members ran down on us, and

---

[7]Here is what ZG said elsewhere about Captain Sid: "At the start of the 1920 season I found myself sadly handicapped by having no boat nor boatman. . . . All the veteran boatmen were secured by contracts to other anglers, so I was compelled to take up one of the younger men. I decided upon Captain Sid Boerstler, and my choice turned out to be fortunate. Boerstler was considered the most expert engineer on the island, and an intelligent and willing young man who, under the training of Lone Angler Wiborn, R. C. and myself, very rapidly developed into a splendid boatman. To his credit for 1920 went the largest broadbill swordfish and the greatest number of marlin, records that assuredly established his reputation."

("The Gladiator of the Sea," *Outdoor America*, March, 1920).

[8]Using a kite to skip the bait well away from a boat's wake was a technique developed by Captain "Tuna George" Chase Farnsworth in the first decade of this century.

[9]Jimmy W. Jump was the only individual in Tuna Club history ever to earn all six of the big-game buttons commemorating outstanding angling achievements.

[10]Harry W. Adams and A. W. Hooper were both exceptional anglers. Adams is one of nine Tuna Club members ever to earn five buttons, but he remained unhappy to the day of his death that club

circled us three times. Before twelve o'clock, half-a-dozen angling boats had run close enough to us to wave congratulatory encouragement. The steamer *Avalon* leaving San Pedro at ten o'clock passed us before noon, and the captain waved to us from the bridge. There were fifteen hundred tourists on board and surely half of them saw us. We saw the crier with his megaphone calling attention to us.

This swordfish leaped twice, once clear out, which jump I photographed. R. C. fought the fish with slow steady powerful strain, never relaxing it. I work on a swordfish in spells: I pull a while and then rest a while, and sometimes I let the rod lie on the gunwale a moment. Adams, who is the most powerful angler of the Tuna Club, says if he cannot whip a fish in four hours, he lets him go. Perhaps that is both wise and humane. Jump fights a fish so strenuously that he claims he soon uses up his strength. All anglers work differently, and any method is good, if the swordfish is caught. To the great majority of anglers it may seem unreasonable to place swordfishing in a class by itself—by far the most magnificent sport in the world with rod and reel. Yet I do not hesitate to make this statement and believe I can prove it. All swordfish fight differently. A swordfish is changeable. That is the beauty of his gameness.

Very few anglers have caught broadbill swordfish. The sport is young at this writing. R. C. had been years trying to catch a broadbill, without success. He has had many battles. So this fish, the first hooked in forty days, meant a great deal to R. C. He worked four hours before he began to tire. From that time the fish began gradually to wear R. C. out, although he was certainly wearing the fish out.

About two o'clock the westerly wind sprang up and white water began to show. By four, long swells were running and big white-crested combers lifted the boat. It is always a terrible job to fight a broadbill in rough water, for every swell helps the fish.

At four thirty, the steamer *Avalon* bore down on us again on her return

rules prohibited women from joining. As late as March 1941, he pleaded their cause by letter from his death bed. By contrast, A. W. Hooper was a confirmed misogynist who could not even stand to see women visit the club! In the summer of 1909, he fished unsuccessfully for bluefin tuna but insisted that he was to be notified immediately if the fish showed up after he went home to Boston. They did, and exactly 23 hours after getting off a train from California, he reboarded one for California. He still didn't catch a tuna that year, and he was at least $15,000 poorer 14 years later when he finally caught his first bluefin. Then he went beserk and caught 80 "blue button fish" from June to mid-September, 1923. Ironically, had he stayed in Massachusetts and pioneered the tuna fishing available to him there, he might have caught fish many times larger than his biggest Pacific bluefin.

trip to the mainland, and she came closer, so that we could see and hear the passengers. Again the captain waved to us.

Wearily R. C. toiled at the rod, sweaty, dirty, green of face, with bulging neck. Capt. Sid grew sea-sick, irritable, and tired of endlessly turning the wheel, and throwing the clutch in and out. I was sore all over from hanging on to the boat. I helped R. C. by holding the revolving chair that wheeled in the rough sea. He had the best of tackle, especially the magnificent Coxe reel. The line, a specially made 24,[11] with breaking strain of sixty-five pounds, apparently was unbreakable. But it was wearing. The swordfish grew so tired he would not swim. Once we thought he was dead. But when R. C. pumped him up close to the boat he wagged his tail and went away. In that sea his dead weight was almost impossible to lift.

The hours wore away. So did R. C. So did the line. But we all thought we had a good chance to capture this fish. The whole latter part of the fight was made near the end of the line, perhaps a hundred feet of it, and it gradually wore, until at 7:35 that night it snapped. Ten hours and five minutes!

R. C. collapsed then, and assuredly showed the effects of that long battle. Today his hands, arms, back and legs are swollen, and very sore. Yet he was in fine condition at the outset of this struggle. Otherwise, of course, it would have been useless to attempt it.

This swordfish probably weighed somewhere between four and five hundred pounds. In that rough sea he was unbeatable. Perhaps if we had been fortunate enough to have had smooth water R. C. might have whipped him. But the job would have been tremendous.

---

[11] This refers to the number of threads in a linen fishing line which should test at three pounds breaking strength per wet thread, or 72 pounds breaking strength for a 24-thread line under actual angling conditions. When ZG says 65 pounds, he is referring to the line's dry breaking strength.

"THREE BROADBILL SWORDFISH"

Introduction

Zane Grey had few preconceived notions about what constituted proper angling. Although he bowed to tradition in calling fly fishing for Atlantic salmon "the highest art of angling," he had his doubts, especially after he caught his first steelhead in Oregon. ZG could not see how Atlantic salmon could be stronger or more acrobatic on a fly, or the setting for the sport more spectacular than sea-run rainbow trout and the cascading rivers of the Pacific Northwest.

Zane Grey became an angling pioneer both because he never liked doing what other people were doing—he preferred to initiate fads, not follow them—and because he was reluctant to return to any angling area unless it satisfied two conditions: abundance and unpredictability. That is why he kept a home on Catalina Island even after he resigned from the Tuna Club. Back in the 1920s, Catalina offered the best all-around swordfishing anywhere in the world. The seas were generally more calm than in other places swordfish roamed, and this calmness made it possible not only to find the finning fish but to fight them without having to fight heavy seas as well.

Zane Grey wanted to be able to see fish, and he saw swordfish almost every day he went for them off Catalina. If they proved difficult to hook and land, so much the better, for that made the achievement of catching one that much more exclusive. In ten years of fishing off Catalina, Zane Grey landed twenty-four swordfish and his brother, R. C., caught eighteen. Those records for daytime swordfishing with rod and reel have never been matched.

However, in the early 1970s, night fishing with "light sticks" to attract

Ernest Hemingway once noted that the only records that matter—the only records that can never be broken—are "firsts." Thus, while all of Zane Grey's many world records are no longer recognized by the International Game Fish Association, this picture shows a record that will never be taken away from him: the first broadbill swordfish ever caught on rod and reel in New Zealand waters.

the swordfish was pioneered by the Webb brothers of Fort Lauderdale, Florida. By the end of that decade overfishing by both recreational fishermen and commercial longliners using light sticks had greatly reduced the odds of any daytime angler catching a broadbill in either the Atlantic or Pacific. In 1973, there were still fewer than five hundred people in angling history who had ever caught a broadbill on rod and reel. By 1983, although countless thousands of people have now caught broadbill, the number of anglers who have stalked, hooked, and landed a swordfish by day is still less than five hundred.

GWR

THREE

BROADBILL SWORDFISH

August 21, 1923, was a cool, dark, windy and not encouraging morning. I was tired out and listless, and did not begin to look for swordfish as early as usual. At ten o'clock Thad[1] sighted one. We ran down on this fellow in a rather lumpy sea—and marvelous to relate soon found ourselves hooked to him. I was amazed, incredulous. The swordfish ran under the boat, taking nearly all the line. Fortunately he stopped, and we backed up on him, so I could recover the line. Then a fight began—slow, laborious, plodding, strenuous. At first I did not work to excess, because I hoped he would tangle up in the leader.[2] But we cannot have so much luck as that. I worked harder and harder, and after a couple of hours began to feel tired. The fish did nothing spectacular. He sounded once, taking half the line. But for the most part he stayed under the boat, comparatively close. It was pump and reel. Sometimes he would rise to the surface, and then we would back down on him while I recovered line. The time came when he grew slower and more sluggish. I went my limit. Dozens of times I got the double line over the reel!

It took four hours and a half to haul him to the boat. He came in tail first, pretty much exhausted. He was hooked far back. Sid gaffed him well, but had to use a second hook. Then he and Thad fought the fish on the gaffs. Even after we hauled him up on block and tackle, he was alive

---

[1] Captain Boestler's mate.
[2] This is not a confession many modern outdoor writers would be willing to make. A tangled and, therefore, drowned or drowning fish is a relatively easy one to land. Most writers would rather have you believe they beat a quickly-yielding fish through their strength of arms and force of character. ZG's confession reveals the mingled dread and awe with which he confronted each new swordfish battle.

for a long time. A long slender swordfish, beautifully built, with enormous rapier-like sword, and high dorsal. Murphy[3] said these were the finest he had seen. I judged his weight at 350, but I was badly off. He weighed only 262 pounds. He was 11 feet 5 inches long, his girth measured 44 inches, and his tail 37½ inches.

August 22nd was a perfect swordfish day. We were on the swordfish banks by 10 o'clock, and at 10:15 Thad sighted number one for the day. He would not bite.

Then I began to pick up swordfish. We worked several, one of which was a most magnificent fish that I saw plainly. He was 12 feet long, and as large around as a barrel. We ran close to him, and his color, his size, his terrifying sword, and the motion of reserved power, all fascinated me to the limit.

The last one I sighted at 11 o'clock took the bait and was hooked. A battle had begun. He was not a sluggish fish like that of yesterday. He ran, and made the surface six times. We tried our level best to chase him and get to close quarters. Every time I got the double line over the reel. But he would sink at the approach of the boat. Then for an hour he fought deep down, and the last of this period was most exciting. I drew him fairly close, right under the boat, and suddenly he made a curvish rush, upward, across under us and away. Swift as a flash! I am sure that move was a threatening one. After that I worked to the limit on him, and in two hours or more he sounded. The line slipped off yard on yard. I let him run. When four hundred feet were off he slowed up, and gradually went slower to the five hundred length. At this he stopped, and held that place without even a jerk for five minutes. This roused my hopes, and when I could wait no longer I began to pump and reel. The line came in by inches, and the effort was great. After a little I could get more line at each wind. The weight was tremendous, but dead. I felt more intense, and could hardly contain myself. When I saw the double line come out of the water, quite some distance from the boat, I let out a yell. And I worked harder. The strain was difficult to keep. At last I had the double line over

[3]*Sic transit gloria.* It is touching that Zane Grey refers to such angling giants and authorities of his day as Mr. Murphy, as though we all know who he means, and as though ZG expected the accomplishments of such pioneers to be remembered by younger anglers eager to establish their own lifetime reputations. L. G. Murphy developed probably the best line of salt-water fishing rods in his generation. In 1908, Gilmour Sharp and Murphy guided by George Farnsworth were the first anglers ever to explore the marine recreational potential of Baja California. This trip became the model for ZG's own piscatorial wanderings to Panama, the Galapagos, and Tahiti. Captain Farnsworth, who was arguably the greatest blue-water guide of all time, wrote that "L. G. Murphy was the most consistent and possibly the best angler ever to fish in Catalina waters. No matter where he was, he was always on the job. He never at any time used a harness." Murphy was 83 years old the summer he admired ZG's swordfish.

Zane Grey favored heavy tackle for heavy fish. He said it was more humane, hence more sporting, to take fish with equipment giving you half a chance of landing them. Contrariwise, it was unsporting to use tackle so light that an exhausted fish eventually broke away, trailing half a reel of line, to die a lingering death. Here we see ZG and his good friend "Lone Angler" Wiborn transferring some heavy line from a huge reel (probably made by Arthur Kovaloski) to the smaller Vom Hofe on the rod in Lone Angler's hand.

the reel, and then hope was born in me. I had him coming. Then I saw a green-white fish shape coming closer, clearer, and next the leader came out to Sid. I leaped up, threw off my drag, and leaned over as Sid heaved on the leader. The fish was slowly wagging. But he was tired out. He came up. And Sid plunged the gaff into him. We expected a great thrashing, but he made no fuss, and we soon had him fast.

I calculated him also 350 pounds, and as we ran back to Avalon he seemd to grow. But to my amaze he weighed only 298. His length was 10 feet 8½ inches, girth 48 inches, sword 44½ inches and tail 34 inches. Time 2¼ hours.

August 31st was a warm calm morning, with high pale fog, and broken places showing pale blue sky. The sea was smooth dark gray. It looked like wind would soon come. We ran the usual course and gradually there was an improvement in the already good conditions. Thad sighted a swordfish three miles off Long Point. We worked him well, but he did not care to associate with us.

We ran on to the center of the channel, and were soon lost in the fog. We could see only two or three miles all around and were absolutely alone. The sea lightened and the sun shone through diffused high fog. The water was like a vast heaving opal, absolutely without ripple. I said: "If there are any broadbills we will see some." And right after that I sighted my first. We worked him. Then I saw my second. We left the first to go to the other, and he would not stay up for us. While waiting for him to come up I sighted my third—a goodly distance off, big fin out, moving so majestically. We ran for him, and on our first approach everything went fine, and we had him hooked.

He began to run off fast and deep. And he made the reel whizz. I took off the drag, and then the line flew. I hoped he would stop. He was sounding deep, and that means a swordfish cannot or does not stay long deeper than 400 or 500 feet. The pressure must be tremendous.[4] R. C., Sid and Thad stood by, watching the line slip off and they looked dubious.

When he had taken 1000 feet R. C. said: "If he goes much farther it's goodnight!" I saw the line straightening out somewhat back of the boat, and I told Sid to throw in the clutch. That, and the fact that the swordfish slowed up, saved the remainder of my line. I began to reel in a few feet every pump. Then, as the boat gathered momentum, I reeled in faster, and soon began to recover a good bit of line. I breathed freer. I mean I breathed, for before that I was breathless! In a few minutes more I had recovered all but a couple hundred feet, and felt safe for the moment.

I then set down to hard work on him. With a powerful drag I hauled away when he slowed up, and when he plunged or sounded I let off my strain. He came near the surface once. Mostly his action was deep, heavy, and slow. He did not make any more long fast runs. We had to follow where he led us, and thus we worked inshore several miles. After the first hour R. C. said: "Well, he must be hooked good, for you sure handed it to

---

[4]Anthropocentrically, a good many sea anglers imagine that all fishes feel water pressure the way we do, while, in fact, a species like the swordfish regularly ranges from the surface down to a 1,000 or more feet without any ill effect.

Pictures of jumping broadbill swordfish are rare because relatively few are caught today in the daytime when fast shutter speeds and fine lenses can record their sometimes spectacular leaps. This was one of two dozen broadbill that Zane Grey caught off Catalina in the 1920s.

him!'' I began myself to feel that I had the hook in for keeps, and I increased the drag and also my efforts.

Somewhere round the end of the second hour I was growing hot, wet, and tired. So I rested, while the fish slowly took line off the reel.

After I had put on the harness, and got my wind back, and the ache out of my hands, I began on him again. Slow and strong I worked him up. He would run off the line fifty or one hundred feet. Then I'd haul him back. All the time, of course, Thad or Sid ran the boat to help me recover line, as much as possible. He was what we call a plugger. Three times I got the double line over the reel, and on the last I felt I could almost hold him. That woke me to renewed efforts. After this time I kept him close to the boat, and many times got the double line back on the reel.

R. C., Thad and Sid indulged in all kind of foolish happy talk—speculation as to his weight—how soon we could fly the flag—what the crowd would say, for all the world like three boy fishers. But it pleased me, though I reprimanded them. "We haven't got this bird yet!" I concluded. Still I could not kill their loquacious optimism.

A remarkable feature of this fight was that R. C. sighted five more broadbills near us, and two that jumped. We had swordfish round us for two whole hours. It was wonderful, inspiring. "Finest day for swordfish this whole year!" I sweated and I ached, and I doubted, and fought off hope, but all the same I was happy and thrilled.

The perfect weather, the big fish on my line, the sense of long hard patience rewarded, the openness and loneliness and beauty of the sea—these made the time fly, and pangs were nothing.

Another fishing boat ran up on us toward the end of the fight, and watched us through glasses. After a long time the anglers in it became aware of swordfish around, and they evidently tried to get a bite. The last we saw of them was when they were endeavoring to fly a kite over a swordfish. I hoped they would hook one, but I knew the chances were one thousand to one that they could do it in such a manner.[5]

The slow and slower resistance of this swordfish inspired me to a final spurt. I went at him again, not fast, but steadily and as powerfully as I could, hoping to draw him near the boat before I gave out. I would pump, reel, and then shut down on the line with both thumbs. Sometimes the line slipped under them, but for the most part I held him.

It took thirty minutes of this to get the double line over the reel. Then I held to the limit of my strength, and hauled the leader up to Sid's eager hands. The swordfish sheered off to the right (my right) and turning with a slow ponderous plunge he passed the stern. Sid just reached him with the gaff, somewhere above the tail. The hold held, and there was a sounding splash, and then a commotion. But he was not wicked on the gaff as some are. Sid and Thad held him, and soon had a rope round his tail. I got up and had a look at him. He was beautiful—purple, bronze, silver, and a perfectly shaped swordfish. R. C. let out a whoop, which was a signal for all of us to whoop. All the rest of the long ride back, and the entrance to Avalon Bay, the blowing of the whistle, the huge crowd coming from everywhere, and lastly the weighing of the fish—these were matters of joy that only a swordfish angler can appreciate.

This swordfish must have been a very pugnacious and savage fellow, for he had 25 scars on one side, and almost as many on the other. It was

---

[5]Swordfish generally feed deep. They come to the surface probably to enjoy its greater warmth which some biologists feel may aid the fish's digestion. Whatever the reason, swordfish do not feed actively on the surface, and they often have to be tricked into thinking they have stunned the angler's bait by slackening the line and letting the bait sink near the somnolent predator. A kite-rigged bait is in constant motion at the surface, and only the most hungry or cantankerous swordfish would slash at a bait skipping over the waves.

amazing to see these signs of his battles. Some were very old and indistinct, some healed over, and some quite recent.

The fish weighed 360 pounds. His length was 11 feet 5 inches, girth 49 inches, bill 3 feet 8¾ inches and his tail 3 feet 2½ inches.

My boy, Loren, six years old, went with Takahashi[6] up on the mountain with glasses to see if they could find us out on the ocean. They saw us coming with the big red and white flag flying. Loren took off his shoes, so to run better, and he and Takahashi ran all the way down the mountain, through town, out on the dock, so to be there when we got in.

I saw Loren in the front of a gang of wildly excited youngsters. His face was wonderful. Awe, delight, wonder! Then I lost sight of him. When it was all over, and I was walking up the street alone, a cold little hand was slipped into mine. Loren had caught up with me. He was limping and carrying his shoes. He babbled incoherently. Who knows? Maybe this incident made him a great fisherman. He could do worse. He could scarcely walk, so lame was he. "The crowd—walked—on my feet!" he said. Later Takahashi told me about their run down the mountain. And I was vastly proud of my little son.

---

[6]George Takahashi was Zane Grey's cook and for twenty years accompanied the writer and his family on many of their hunting and fishing expeditions. After ZG died in 1939, the family lived less extravagantly and Takahashi was let go. However, the Greys tried to stay in touch and were horrified to learn during World War II that Takahashi was in a concentration camp for American citizens of Japanese ancestry. The Greys tried to intervene but were unsuccessful. After the war, Takahashi worked as a Pullman porter before the Greys lost contact.

"PERMIT—A RARE GAME FISH OF THE CORAL SHOALS"

Introduction

Unlike most of his contemporaries who went to the Florida Keys to catch sailfish, Zane Grey saw that what made this archipelago unique was not the proximity of the Gulf Stream nor even the fabulous coral reefs, but its thousands of square miles of shallow water flats. ZG knew he could catch bigger billfish off California, so why should he pound himself purple in the Gulf Stream when calm water and angling more like hunting could be found a few hundred yards from his cabin door on Long Key?

Most fishermen like to make trips back to the same areas for the same species season after season. Zane Grey did some of this, but his restless temperament kept him looking for new experiences with new fishes even when he was angling in already familiar waters. Unfortunately, mixed with his restlessness was an impatience—not to say, intolerance—of less intrepid sportsmen who didn't see things his way. Since it was evident to Zane Grey that any gamefish of the coral shoals could swim circles around the most vigorous fresh-water fish, how could any angler remain loyal to black bass or trout if he had the money and leisure to visit the Florida Keys?

ZG's impatience shows up in the following story from the March 1925 issue of *Outdoor America* in which he introduces his friend, Will Dilg, and the rest of the angling world to a practically unknown species called the permit.

GWR

PERMIT—A RARE
GAME FISH OF THE
CORAL SHOALS

The first specimen of this remarkable fish to come under my observation was caught at Long Key, Florida, during the winter of 1922, by J. A. Wiborn. I have written elsewhere of the extraordinary fight we had with this fish. We were fishing for bonefish from a canoe. When Wiborn hooked this permit we, of course, took it for a bonefish of great size and speed, for it shot off the shoals with the velocity of a bullet. I pulled up anchor and paddled strenuously for a mile before Wiborn could recover any line. We never would have known what this fish was had we not been able to follow it swiftly in a light canoe; and after a long battle he conquered it. I was exhausted and Wiborn's hands and arms were almost paralyzed.

At first I thought the fish was an African pompano, which it much resembled.[1] Some years before I had caught one of these giant pompano weighing thirty-five pounds. It was taken trolling out on the reef. I was not, however, by any means sure that this queer fish really was an African pompano. It weighed twenty-one pounds, and excited a good deal of curiosity at Long Key, where Parke, the taxidermist, finally classified it as a permit. We learned that a permit was occasionally taken at Key West, and often at Boca Grande, by tarpon fishermen who were still-fishing with crab-bait for tarpon. Crowninshield, one of the Long Key Club

---

[1] The African pompano (*Alectis crinitus*) and the permit (*Trachinotus falcatus*) are closely related members of the family Carangidae—the jacks, scads and pompanos. Both African pompano and permit are excellent food and game fish, but while permit prefer to forage over the flats and around shallow wrecks and other obstructions, the African pompano frequents "ocean holes" in deeper water.

anglers, said the permit was sometimes caught at Boca Grande, and "put up a devil of a fight, even on tarpon rods."

This, of course, excited my interest, and thereafter I kept a sharp lookout for permit on the bonefish shoals. But I did not see another that year. The next winter, fishing with my brother, R. C., on the No. 2 bonefish flat, I saw a large silver fish with a black ribbon-like fin, go after my bait. I recognized it as a permit before I hooked it. This fish took us off into deep water, where I eventually subdued it, no easy task on the light bonefish tackle. It weighed fourteen and three-quarter pounds.

R. C. was so keenly enthusiastic about this permit, the first he had seen, that he wrote his version of its capture. Then later the same season my boatman Sid,[2] fishing with R. C., hooked a fish in very shallow water, and it gave him a most exciting and strenuous time. It turned out to be a permit weighing seven and a half pounds. R. C. and Sid testified that it had more speed, strength and endurance than any bonefish they had ever hooked. This corroborated my own estimate.

The next winter at Long Key I saw a number of permit and learned more about them. Captain Newton Knowles, my boatman that season, was a native of Key West, and he had spent his life on the coral shoals of the Florida Keys. He said there were plenty of permit, but owing to their extreme shyness they were seldom seen in the shallow water, let alone caught. He had speared them up to forty pounds; and one of that weight was hard to kill. Like bonefish, the permit was a crab-eater. He did not frequent as shallow water as the bonefish because his shape would not allow it. He is built like a shield, almost as high as he is long.

During this season, while standing in the bow of my skiff, poling along with watchful eye alert for bonefish, I saw at different times several pairs of permit. They blazed under the water and the wavy black fin and deep-forked tail showed distinctly. At Bowleg Key that March, I had the great good fortune to be with Knowles when he sighted a school of a dozen or fifteen of these fish, all larger than any I had seen. In each instance the permit worked away into deep water again. In April, while fishing for tarpon with Captain Thad Williams[3] near Man-of-War Bush, we espied a school of permit, all swimming with long black fins out of water. Captain Williams was surprised at my excitement. He told me he had seen thousands of permit "finning" that way off Cape Romano.[4]

---

[2]This is Captain Sid Boerstler with whom ZG fished in Catalina and who went with ZG to Nova Scotia in the summer of 1924 to help him land his world record bluefin tuna.
[3]This is the same man who was Captain Boerstler's mate in the previous story about broadbill swordfishing off Catalina. Obviously, *Captain* Williams has moved up in the world in the intervening year.
[4]A Florida cape about midway between Boca Grande, where Captain Williams had taken a party tarpon fishing, and Long Key.

But he did not remember of ever seeing any caught on a rod, though they were often taken in nets.

During February, 1924, I had another and more intimate experience with a permit. R. C. and I, in separate skiffs, were fishing for bonefish at the picturesque point three miles above Long Key Camp.

I had fished for a long time without any luck. Then it chanced that, in the spirit of contrariness which attacks an angler at times, I put on the red tail-end of an enormous soldier crab.[5] It was too big for the biggest bonefish. As I stood up to cast I saw the black fin of a permit a hundred feet out. He was working up the coast. I got out of the skiff and made a long cast far ahead of him, so as not to scare him. Then I waited in most tense excitement.

It appeared he wavered to and fro, somewhat in line with my bait. Directly he must have caught scent of it. I was positive of this, for he could not have seen it. And the sense of smell is powerfully developed in some fish. Anyway he went right to my bait, and as apparently he nosed about it, he elevated part of his forked tail out of the water. Sight of this surely gave me successive thrills. Then I felt the line move very slightly. How hard to wait! But I did so until I felt the line move again.

Then with every nerve tingling I swept up my rod. It came hard against a solid weight. The water swirled, then opened with a thump, and its green clearness turned to muddy yellow.

Next came the rush. As my line hissed through the water I yelled lustily for R. C., who was below me. Still there seemed no hope of stopping or holding the fish. The wisdom of using a long line was here manifest. I had three hundred and fifty yards of the best nine-thread line, and if I had been using anything shorter or lighter he would have broken off. He took three hundred yards in one magnificent run.

Luckily the shallower water compelled him to turn. Thus I had him broadside. He made a ridge on the surface and he went so fast the line made a loud hiss cutting the water. By the time R. C. got to me the permit was splashing at a great rate, throwing up the mud, and cavorting around in a manner to arouse my encouragement. He had been denied the straight long rush that usually meant freedom. I put on all the strain I could with the five-ounce rod, and I began to try to recover line. I got it half back when he made another run. Dragging all that tight line must have slowed him up. At any rate I stopped him, and began again to pump and wind. When he was broadside on, I could do nothing.

I had to hold a very tight line to keep it from fouling on the bottom. This part of the battle, with over two hundred yards of line out, did not

---

[5]Probably a species of hermit crab.

Zane Grey and his fellow sportsmen/conservationists of the 1920s understood only part of the problem of perpetuation. They knew that commercial fishermen made serious inroads on various resources, but they denied that sportsmen could. Furthermore, fish killed but not used by sportsmen were not to be compared with commercial overkills and waste. However, the irony of using permit as trophies or photographic models but not food is that this species is one of the most exquisitely delicious fish in salt water.

inspire me with confidence. And at last, seeing if I let him stay out there I would surely lose him, I gave that tackle a very risky trial. It held, however, and gradually I worked the permit inshore, where by careful handling I eventually beached him. I had taken no account of time, but the fact that my left forearm was dead and my right hand almost paralyzed testified to the sustained exertion. I had never had a moment of rest.

This permit was exceedingly beautiful, an exquisite shade of silver opal not possible to describe. The black markings were the most wonderful I ever saw on a fish, and resembled the loveliest of Japanese decorative art. He had great solemn purple eyes, a massive head, snub-nosed like the gamy salmon, and a small mouth, leather-lipped, I might say, and jaws that indicated great crushing power. He weighed seventeen pounds, and, as far as I was concerned, established the sport of permit fishing as exceedingly more difficult than that of bonefishing.[6]

A few years before such a fact would have seemed incredible. But there is always a greater fish to strive for—always strange new creatures to study and love and fight. It would be much better to limit oneself to the two former activities but somehow with me all three are synonymous.

Several days later in the season I had my friend Will Dilg, president of the Izaak Walton League, in the canoe with me. Dilg was ill. The long toil and worry of the League battle to win the Upper Mississippi Game and Fish Preserve had worn him out.[7] He had on former occasions at Long Key tried and failed to catch a bonefish. It was not any fault of mine. He was so used to the smashing strike of black bass that he could not feel the infinitesimally delicate touch of our silver bullet of the shoals. He had listened for years about the superlative powers of bonefish and shouted back and raved at me, black bass, black bass!

This time, I did succeed in guiding him into bonefish after bonefish strike until the day when he hooked one. Holy-mackeli! When Dilg, after a chaotic struggle, brought that bonefish to where I could net it, he was a well man. After that he fished me nearly to death. What were tides to him? He caught two more bonefish, then hooked a big one that broke his tackle—I mean my tackle—and left him breathless and stunned.

No longer did I have to listen to verses and sermons on our bronze-back fresh-water warriors. Strange to note he ceased asking me about those six and seven-pound small-mouth bass that I used to fight so hard in the swift rocky riffles of the Delaware River.

The fates were against him. He hooked a permit! Of all the weird and wild and whirling exhibitions I ever saw! He was not on familiar terms with a canoe. I managed, by Herculean efforts of strength, and Hiawathaian maneuvers of skill, to keep the canoe upright. And eventually he subdued the permit. It was a small one, in fact the smallest I ever saw. Dilg gazed at it in stupefaction.

"Hey," he gasped, at last, "did that—little fish—put up that fight?"

"Why, you landed him very easily," I replied, mildly. "Wait till you hook a big permit."

---

[6]Still true today, whether using spinning or conventional gear, but especially fly tackle. Probably fewer than one hundred anglers have ever taken permit on a fly.

[7]A devoted smoker, Will Dilg was dying of throat cancer. His increasingly long stays in hospitals cost him his control of the Izaak Walton League, and he was removed from office the year after this article appeared and died a year after that on March 27, 1927.

Dilg recklessly waved his rod—I mean my rod—one of my best, for he had ruined all the poor ones. "Lemme go home!" he wailed. "I love black bass. And I *can't* be a traitor!"[8]

A remarkable thing in connection with the capture of these permit was the fact that, up to this time, these were the only ones ever caught there. Thompson and Fisher,[9] both long-experienced and expert bone-fishermen, had never to their knowledge ever had a bite from one. I decided the reason for this lay in the fact that R. C. and I always chose a different depth of water and kind of coral shoal from the other anglers. We did not imagine we knew more; it was just a development with us. An interesting thing in this connection was Thompson's remark that he had lately taken more and more to deeper water. Some day he will hook a big permit.

This season of 1924 I left Long Key early to fish at Key West, which place Mr. L. P. Schutt believes has a great future, as do I. Before we went, I had a talk with Meisselbach[10] about permit.

"Gus," as he is known to his friends—and any angler who can call this fine gentle-souled man his friend is indeed fortunate—had always taken very kindly to my hints about bonefish. As a matter of fact I take pride in imagining that I helped to make Gus Meisselbach the great angler he has become.[11] Any way I gave him a long talk on permit, and certainly stirred his enthusiasm. He loved to fish the places R. C. and I frequented, and he had developed ability to find new places of his own. He loved the loneliness of the shoals, the sun and wind, the clouds and birds; and I believed he had the patience to catch a permit. So I told him what to do and he said he would do it.

Spring found me at home writing. I looked for a letter from Meissel-bach, but it did not come. So I concluded he had not had the luck to hook a permit. In July I went to Avalon, in August to Nova Scotia, Oregon in September, during which time mail had little access to me. But upon

---

[8]Although H. L. Mencken observed that loyalty is the first quality of a dog, it was the essential ingredient of the many fraternal orders that flourished during Mencken's day. Just as Will Dilg could not be a "traitor" to the black bass, Zane Grey could not be a traitor to Will Dilg. When Dilg lost the presidency of the Izaak Walton League in April 1926, Zane Grey resigned his membership in protest.

[9]Two members of the Long Key fishing fraternity.

[10]A. F. "Gus" Meisselbach was the designer and manufacturer of an extensive line of fishing reels. One of the most popular models for Florida flats fishing was Meisselbach's No. 620 "Okeh" level-wind. With an ivory handle, this brass and German silver reel retailed in 1925 for fifteen dollars.

[11]Like most manufacturers of sporting equipment, Meisselbach had less opportunity to use the tackle he made than the people who bought it. However, Meisselbach was a better angler than this unnecessarily patronizing remark of ZG's indicates.

my return home in October I found the long-expected letter from Meisselbach.

That letter was a document, a classic, a joy. The part of it, however, that pertained to this story, was the wonderful news about the permit. Gus had caught five over ten pounds. Of his first catch he wrote much that was thrilling and amusing, but I shall quote only a passage or two. It will serve to corroborate my estimate of this rare fish, and also to give an inkling of what a grand old fisherman Meisselbach is.

". . . I also remembered your advice that if I should hook a permit, to have my boatman pull up anchor and chase him. But I was alone in my skiff when I hooked this first permit. . . . I remember every move of myself and fish. . . . Not for the longest time was I aware of having hooked a permit although I felt him to be a tremendous fighter. Then he began to circle, and finally I saw he was a permit. I began asking the good Lord to be good to me and see that I wouldn't lose him, and later on when I got him near the boat and was afraid something would give way, I further besought the Lord to see to it in that event I could endure to be a good loser."

Hail to this Izaak Walton! That is the beautiful spirit for an angler. But Meisselbach got this permit and he said he was as proud of it as I must have been at the capture of my 758-pound tuna.

Later in his letter Meisselbach stated that all five permit made very much longer and harder runs than bonefish. And he said he wondered if it was not a fact that many of those bonefish he could not stop were not really permit. They were indeed! R. C. and I can testify to that.

I cannot find very much information in scientific books about the permit. What Goode has to say is very interesting:[12]

"The African Pompano, *T. goreensis*, originally described from the island of Gorea, on the west coast of Africa, resembles in general form the Round Pompano, though somewhat more elongate, while the head is larger. . . . The anterior rays of the dorsal and anal extend beyond the middle of the fin, if laid backward. In the number of the fin rays it corresponds most closely with the Round Pompano. . . . It is the largest of Pompanoes. Dr. Velie obtained two large specimens in West Florida, and in 1879 Mr. Blackford sent to the National Museum a giant of the same species, taken at Jupiter Inlet . . . weighing twenty-three pounds. It has since become evident that the species figured by Girard in the ichthyol-

---

[12]George Brown Goode first published his *American Fishes* in 1887 when the scientific names of many members of the pompano family were still developing and when the permit was thought to be the same species as the African pompano.

ogy of the United States and Mexican boundary, under the name *Dolio-don carolinus*, is really *Trachynotus goreensis*, and that its occurrence in the Gulf of Mexico is not unusual . . . being known at Key West as the Permit."

I quote several items from Gregg:[13]

"Permit or Pompano. This large Pompano, which attains a weight of twenty-five pounds, is not uncommon along the Keys."

(Report of Hugh M. Smith, U. S. Commission, 1895.)

"Key West Permit, or Permit of Key West, *Trachinotus goodei*."

(Evermann & Bean, report to U. S. Commission, 1896.)

"Permit, *Trachinotus goodei*, J. & E. This species is not very common about Key West. It reaches a weight of forty pounds."

All of which attests to rather sparse and contrary information about this singular fish. That he is a remarkably shy, elusive fish, and unequalled as to gameness, I can certainly testify. But I do not believe the permit of the coral shoals is a fish for all anglers to aspire to catch, even most of the bonefishermen. He is too hard to find, too difficult to catch. To the angler, however, who is forever yearning for the almost unattainable, I recommend the pursuit of the permit.

---

[13]William H. Gregg published *Where, When, and How to Catch Fish on the East Coast of Florida* in 1902. By quoting sources more than 20 years old, ZG is stacking the deck in favor of the permit as a mysterious species. Actually, by 1925, a little more was known about the biology and ecology of this fish, but to obtain such information, ZG would have had to read through the scientific literature at a major library or museum, and he had little enough time for his lucrative fiction and obviously less for an article for which he was paid nothing.

"BIRDS OF THE SEA"

Introduction

In the January 1924 issue of *Outdoor America*, Zane Grey contributed a contentious piece on "Heavy Tackle for Heavy Fish," meaning sword-fish, that could only have been of interest to a few hundred people in all the world, much less the 100,000 members of the Izaak Walton League. Will Dilg and ZG must have had a little heart-to-heart talk in which Grey reminded Dilg that he was not being paid for his contributions to *Outdoor America*, and Dilg reminded Grey that that didn't matter: the League was a sacred cause!

The upshot of their tête-à-tête was a special section in the magazine entitled "Outdoors with Zane Grey." Under this heading are some of ZG's most passionate pleas for conservation, for example, a call to tax all private vehicles used on federal lands and "A Warning to California" (November 1924), as well as some inspired nature reporting on subjects ranging from whales to sea birds.

All his life, Zane Grey wanted reputable scientists to take him and his observations of nature seriously. Unfortunately, most scientists dismissed ZG as a popular hack with no proper educational or employment credentials. The ultimate loser of such jealous snobbery was science itself, for Zane Grey traveled to places and saw things that would be well off natural history's beaten track for at least another 30 years. With a little encouragement, Zane Grey would have fallen all over himself to provide museums with notes and specimens from his far flung expeditions.

One of the few respected naturalists of his day to respond to Zane Grey's plea for recognition was William Henry Hudson. At least this distinguished novelist and ornithologist was courteous enough to re-

spond to ZG's correspondence. In turn, Zane Grey uses this correspondence to lend authority to his own observations of "Birds of the Sea" in
the June 1924 issue of *Outdoor America.*

GWR

BIRDS OF THE SEA

The last letter I received from W. H. Hudson, the English writer and
naturalist, was written with a death-striken hand;[1] and therefore the
more to be treasured were his words: "I was glad to read about the wild
and beautiful birds of your lonely coral reefs."

This message from one of the great golden-mouthed Englishmen
made me feel infinite regret that I had not devoted more study and love to
birds of the sea, as well as to the fish. And I resolved that I would begin at
once to rectify my mistake and make up for lost opportunities.

The birds that inspired Mr. Hudson's letter to me were the boobies and
the man-of-war pelicans, or frigate birds.[2] The natives of Yucatan, who
took me out to coral reefs in the Caribbean called this huge black sea
hawk *rabiahorcado.*

The man-of-war bird preys upon the boobies by stealing their fish,
even to the extent of making them disgorge it. These hereditary foes live
on the same islands and nest together. A striking provision of nature,
however, is manifested in the fact that though the boobie will kill the
young of its enemy, the man-of-war pelican will never hurt the young of
the bird it preys upon.

---

[1] Hudson was born in Buenos Aires of American parents in 1841, and most of his best books have
South American settings, although from 1870, he lived in England. Hudson died in 1922 and a
popular biography of him by Morley Roberts appeared several months before ZG's article and
may have been the reason ZG goes out of his way to refer to his long-distance acquaintance with
the highly respected author of *The Purple Land* (1885), *The Naturalist in La Plata* (1892) and
Green Mansions (1904).

[2] The magnificent frigate bird or man-o'-war (*Fregata magnificens*) and the masked or blue-faced
booby (*Sula dactylatra*) are members of the Pelecaniform order. Therefore, ZG is technically
correct in referring to "man-of-war pelicans."

Although the magnificent frigate bird will harry and rob almost any other bird fishing over bait, frigate birds do little harrassing of their own species and are skilled fishers in their own right. Grey called the frigate "the falcon of the sea."

The mature boobie is a bird larger than a gull, of an exquisite pure white color, with black-tipped wings. He has a long sharp bill. On the wing he is a swift and powerful flier, even stronger than the shearwater of the Pacific. He goes out to sea and returns with a flying fish in his gullet for his young. He sticks his bill down into the wide mouth of his offspring and disgorges the flying fish.[3]

---

[3]In Pelecaniform species, just the opposite occurs: the offspring insert their mandibles into their parents' gullets.

The mature frigate bird is verily the falcon of the sea. He is shiny black with white breast. His sweep of bowed wings reach seven feet across. His tail consists of several long feathers, sometimes folded in a narrow point and at others forked. This frigate bird seems born of the wind. He has the most beautiful flight of any bird I have ever seen. How he sails, floats, soars with never a movement of wings! Like thistledown he rides the wind, yet how perfectly he is master of it. Over the water he glides, sometimes low, mostly high, watching for the return of a boobie. Like a thunderbolt he shoots down. Even the eagle in his magnificent swoop is hardly comparable to this sea bird.

Along the keys of lower Florida the frigate bird is seen occasionally, a smaller bird, not so wide of wing or large of body, yet evidently the same species.[4] His mode of life, however, is different. In the Caribbean he preys off another bird; on the Florida reefs he fishes for himself. And he is a past master at the art. Along these reefs his marvelous sailing flight is even more striking than in Yucatan. Miles he covers with never a movement of wing! Then how he wheels, how he darts! I have seen one swoop down to catch a live fish in his bill. He does not plunge down like an osprey or fish hawk, nor with the plummet drop of the tern; he curves down, swift as light.

One of my boatmen, Captain Knowles, who has lived his life along these reefs, claims the frigate birds devour young turtles. Along the sandy beaches of Cape Sable the big turtles make their nests and lay their eggs, hundreds of them. When these hatch, the little turtles swarm out on the sand. Only a few ever reach the water they were destined for. Wildcats, raccoons, and the voracious man-of-war birds seem to lie in wait for this birthday of the little turtles.[5]

---

[4] A different race possibly but definitely the same species.
[5] This is a true description of an extraordinary event that only in the last decade was finally recorded on film. It is still one of the countless unknown mysteries of nature as to how the magnificent frigate birds know when to gather along the shore for the hatching of the sea turtles.

"THE SEVENTH WAVE"

Introduction

Poor Zane Grey. He was baffled by the Internal Revenue Service's harassment of him. He was a loyal American and he didn't mind paying his fair share of taxes, but he disagreed with what the IRS claimed was his fair share.

ZG resented the fact that other businessmen could deduct such business-related expenses as travel and equipment while he apparently could not. If he had allowed his boatmen to run charters when he wasn't aboard and then taken a share of those profits, ZG would have been able to deduct all the expenses associated with operating those boats, including tackle. As it was, no matter how many articles and books he wrote either on board or inspired by events that occurred while aboard, the IRS categorized his boats and tackle as recreational equipment and, therefore, not deductible.

Likewise, no matter where ZG traveled in the world to gather material for his profitable fiction, the IRS ruled that unless such travel was in a professional group and conference-related, ZG was on a nondeductible holiday, no matter how many stories might come out of a trip.

Eventually ZG became an outdoor writing pioneer in more ways than even he imagined, when his ongoing battles with the IRS eventually led to revisions in the Internal Revenue codes that benefit modern outdoor writers by permitting us to deduct our fishing and hunting expenses. Unfortunately, there remains one large fly in the ointment. If a story, such as "The Seventh Wave," which appeared in the January 1923 issue of what was still called the Izaak Walton League Monthly, is donated to a non-profit organization, the only thing the writer gets to deduct is the

The young man playfully threatened with a coconut at the Long Key Fishing Club in light-hearted days prior to World War I is artist Frank L. Stick who, along with Zane Grey, contributed much time and talent to making *Outdoor America* a powerful voice for conservation in the 1920s.

cost of the paper on which the story is submitted. Not even his time is deductible.

Similarly, an artist such as Frank L. Stick who originally contributed two watercolors to go with the story, is allowed to deduct only the cost of the paints actually used and the two sheets of paper on which the illustrations appear. Of course, if a businessman later gets his hands on such creative material and has it appraised for many hundreds or thousands of dollars, he is allowed to donate the manuscripts and art to a library or museum for the appraised value. But the artist still gets nothing in the way of a tax break.

In an open letter to fellow sportsmen dated July 10, 1926, Zane Grey complained "I gave [Will] Dilg [and the Izaak Walton League] in three years, work that would have amounted to $100,000.00. Frank Stick, the artist, did as much." ZG was boasting about his contributions to conservation, but he was also pleading his case with the IRS whose accountants unctuously replied, "If you can afford to give away so much make-believe money, surely you can afford to give us a comparable share of the real stuff.''

And one does wonder why a fine yarn like "The Seventh Wave" wasn't sold for the several thousand dollars it might have earned in the pulp popular fiction market.

GWR

THE SEVENTH WAVE

A lacranes is a naked surf-beat shingle of the world, a lonely coral-reef off the lonely coast of Yucatan.[1] The name signifies scorpion, and the reef lies with its long tail curled, as if crouching to spring upon the ships that go down to the sea.

The keeper of the lighthouse told me that two of his predecessors had gone insane. But he was happy there; he loved the sea; he loved the mechanical work connected with his wonderful light; he loved to see the circling flash go over the water; he loved to watch the ships pass far out in the night and to feel what his lonely life meant to mariners.

"To stay here," he said, "like that gull there, you must be of the sea."

I saw a beautiful sea-bird skim the shoals and soar aloft to poise on the wind and dart in wild flight across the sand and drop down to breast the waves and wing a wandering course over the reefs.

For hours I strolled along the white beach and picked up shells and seaweed; I marveled at bits of wood and nuts drifting in from some far-off unknown shore; I watched the slender-winged wild-flying sea-fowls. By day I climbed to the top of the lofty lighthouse to look out over the white shoals, the green shallows, the blue lagoons, the deep purple channels, the long tumbling white wall of the barrier reef, and beyond to the dark, heaving restless sea. By night I sat under the circling light and watched the wonderful flashes gleam into the sea. Always I heard the deep crashing boom of the surf on the barrier reef; always the hollow monoto-

---

[1] Arrecife Alacrán lies about 75 miles off the Yucatan peninsula near where the Campeche Bank drops off the edge of the Continental Shelf. Even today, the fishing there is spectacular, but so are the navigational hazards.

nous beat of the waves on the shoals; always the ripples lapping the coral strand. From the open sea the wind brought a low strange murmur and moan. It was incessant and mournful. It was mysterious and sad. I was fascinated by the sea; I never tired of it; day and night I watched and listened.

But I grew lonely.

The keeper of the lighthouse said to me: "You are not of the sea. To stay here you must have it in your blood."

Then he told me a story of his ancestors, people of the sea.

Campeche, a port of Yucatan, was for many years subject to the attacks of buccaneers of the Spanish Main. In 1686 after it had been plundered by Grammont and DeGraaf, two noted rovers of the time, the inhabitants erected round it a wall of stone, which, rising like a white cliff, could be seen far out at sea. That served however, only as a landmark to help guide the pirates through dangerous reefs to the low-lying town.

In the late summer of that year, the brig *Metista* cleared from Vera Cruz with a valuable cargo, made fair sailing to the fringe of the trades, and off the Yucatan Banks almost within sight of the white wall of Campeche, she encountered foul weather and had to turn her nose toward the open sea. She rode out the storm and was getting back on her course when she was run down by a black craft, shot full of holes, sacked and sunk.

Jean Jaurez, quartermaster of the brig, was the only one of the crew whose life was spared, and he, in relating the story, said he was struck down at the wheel, and when he returned to consciousness found himself in the hold of the pirate ship among bales of stolen cargo and coils of ill-smelling rope. He lay there weak and dizzy for a day and a night before learning what disposition was to be made of him; and then he was visited by a French pirate who told him the captain gave him a choice of running the ship through the dangerous channels to Campeche or of having his head split with a cutlass. Jaurez agreed to pilot the ship, meaning to run her on the reefs.

Then he was left alone with scant food and drink and he fell prey to gloomy thoughts. The *Metista* with her gallant crew had gone to the bottom of the sea. He thought of his mother and sister, and saw them climb the Campeche wall to look with anxious glance over the waves. No sail! The *Metista* would never again gleam like a gull against the distant blue, never again bring light to wistful eyes and warmth to loving hearts. Her fate would be a mystery, unless the dead were cast up by the sea.

The pain in Jaurez's throat was as great as that in his head. He choked back the sobs and tried to think no more of home. At length he slept and when he awakened, another night had passed. The bright morning light streamed through the open hatchway. He saw the blue sky above the huge bellying sail of the ship. A breeze whistled through the shrouds. The booms swung and cracked; the rings turned and creaked; the timbers of the vessel groaned. The water roared under the bow. Jaurez discovered he was hungry and thirsty, and, though suffering considerable pain from the bruise on his head, was in no wise incapacitated by his misfortune. He began to revolve in mind the possibilities of the situation and how to meet them. In moving about the hold he almost stumbled over a girl lying outstretched on a tarpaulin. Wildly she started up, and he recognized her as having been one of the few passengers on the *Metista*. He had heard her called Ollone. She had been injured, for there was blood on her face.

"Don't be afraid," he whispered. "I'm not a pirate. I was quartermaster of the *Metista*. . . . Are you hurt?"

"Only a little . . . I ran and was knocked down," she replied. "But, oh! I am frightened. . . . Save me!"

Just then a pair of muscular brown feet appeared on the upper rung of the ladder and a harsh voice called Jaurez.

"Pretend to be badly hurt," whispered Jaurez to the girl, and then moved rapidly away.

He followed the sailor up the ladder and staggered on deck, simulating a weakness that he was far from feeling. The ship was a two-master, canoe-shaped, sharp fore and aft, very old and massive and lay low in the water under an enormous spread of canvas. Long-nosed bronze cannon glittered around the deck. At the tiller stood a sailor of herculean build, naked except for cotton breeches. Then from the deck rose a short broad man—and Jaurez recoiled from the master of the ship. As fixed as if cut in stone was the violence of his face. He questioned Jaurez about the treacherous coast, the low-lying coral reefs, the channel into the bay of Campeche, and lastly about the garrison and defenses of the town. Then he turned to his giant helmsman. Jaurez appeared to have the freedom of the ship and he walked about, but he still kept up his pretense of being half dazed by his injury. He passed some of the black-faced, bare-footed crew, grim and sinister even in slumber. Near the main-mast there was a tarpaulin rigged up to make shade, and under it a fire-box, with charcoal smouldering in a wire grate. Water splashed from the bung-hole of a barrel, and here he quenched his thirst.

The breeze dropped off, as was usually the case in that latitude during noon hours, and there was a long smooth swell with only widely scattered wreaths of white. The helmsman had tacked close into the wind to gain as much as possible on the strong northern drift of the tide. After a while the breeze died altogether. The ship drifted with flapping limp sails. In the glaring heat of mid-day the helmsman slept with his hand on the idle tiller. Porpoises played and long, silver, sharp-jawed fish leaped after sardines,[2] and black-finned sharks basked in the sun, beautiful snow-white boobies soared in graceful low flight. Jaurez knew from the presence of these birds that the ship was near a coral island. The hours passed, silent, monotonous, waiting. Then, as if by magic, the glassy swells wrinkled and dimpled, a dark ripple glided and glanced astern; and farther on appeared a wavering line, ocean-wide, curling with creamy crest, like the bore of an incoming tide. The northeast trade whipped up a white-wreathed sea; and the ship skimmed the waves, slipping over the sea as slick as oil.

The chief called the crew on deck. They were a yawning, stretching, villainous assortment of seamen, none young, all black-browned and fierce. As they sat on the deck to eat they jabbered and laughed aloud, and they made a gloomy crowd.

Jaurez's mind was active with fear and distress. Where was the ship rushing? The whole rigging above him strained under the strong sweep of the wind. The mainsail curved into a deep hollow with a network of rope-shadows thrown by light from the westering sun. The bare feet of sailors made soft padded sounds. Once he saw the chief and his giant

---

[2]Zane Grey is not using *sardine* to refer to a particular herring species suitable for canning, but merely to represent any small fish.

helmsman pacing the deck, and heard one of them say: "The last cruise!" No other words helped Jaurez to interpret the speech.

Toward afternoon the pirate chief ordered a sailor aloft. The man walked up the halyards, gripping the rope with his toes and reaching hand over hand. When half way up he faced the south and uttered a cry that meant he had sighted land.

For a while Jaurez dared not look southward, and when he did, a long white strip gleamed above the swelling blue ocean-line. It was the Campeche wall. He recognized it with passionate protest against his fate. When would he be called to take the tiller? But he did not waver in his resolve to steer the ship upon the reefs. Turning in his despair he moved so that he overlooked a hatchway. He gazed down into the dingy hole and saw some casks that at first seemed only casks, like any other things belonging to the hated ship. But an irresistible attraction which he could not comprehend kept his glance glued to those casks. They were open. They contained coarse black grains. "Powder," he muttered. "The devils have got the powder out for the cannon." Suddenly a rush of hot blood, a flash of divination made him whisper: "Blow up the ship!"

When he regained calmness he knew he had thought to blow up the ship and sacrifice his life to save Campeche. But as his wits returned, it occurred to him to wait till night, set a lighted fuse in the powder, then leap overboard and swim ashore. The ship was five leagues off the coast. The pirate probably meant to go in closer to shore and lay to till morning. Then Jaurez would be put at the wheel.

All at once Jaurez remembered the girl in the hold. He could not blow up the ship with her in it. And a daring purpose flashed over him. His lowered gaze roved about the deck. Near at hand were bits of tarry rope, a fishing line, and an old cork life-preserver! It seemed a miracle that they should be there.[3] With these, and one moment of opportunity he could save Ollone and escape himself, and also send the ship to the bottom. He began to wander about in an apparently aimless manner, stumbling here and there, and at length went down the ladder. In an instant he was kneeling beside the girl. Her hands caught his.

"Can you swim?" he whispered.

"Yes," she replied.

"If you will do as I tell you I can save you."

"Oh! . . . I will!"

---

[3]From Elizabethan theater to the modern novel, melodrama depends on such convenient "miracles."

"Wait and listen. It will be dark before I give you a signal. Wait till you hear something drop into the hold. Then come quickly up the ladder. Do not hesitate. I'll meet you. I'll slip a life-preserver around you and a string over your wrist. Do not speak a word. Then dive into the sea. I'll follow."

Jaurez returned to the deck and adopted a dull lounging position near the mainmast. But his mind was in a ferment. The afternoon dragged by as if it were a thousand years. He drank thirstily but did not eat what was placed before him. At twilight the ship lay to within two leagues of Campeche. Jaurez's sensations were strange; he seemed far off from everything; he felt faint; a little more waiting in suspense would drive him mad. Under drooped eyelids he watched with keen gaze. How slowly the sea darkened! The darkness seemed to come on the great slow swells. The guard who had kept careless and desultory watch on Jaurez wandered aft to join the circle of pirates.

The gloom deepened. The compass-lantern threw a dull flare upon the circle of dark faces. Not a man showed fore of the mainsail. The moment had come. Jaurez arose silently. He saw a dim glow on the sea, showing the tide sweeping shoreward; he saw the faint lights of Campeche beckoning out of the darkness. He thought of the girl he meant to save. And suddenly he felt intensely keen, and strong as he had never known strength.

Then he threw a piece of rope down into the hold. There was a rustle—soft steps—a shadow—and Ollone rose before him slim and straight. Her hands caught him and clung to him. Swiftly he tied the life preserver under her arms; swiftly he noosed the line over her wrist. He thrilled at the level gaze of great dark eyes. Without a sound she glided away from him. Dimly he saw her slender form—lost it—and stood waiting with his heart in his throat. His ear just caught a soft splash. Then the ball of twine in his hand began to revolve.

Steathily Jaurez crawled from the shadow of the bulging sheet of canvas and reaching the fire-box, he picked up a smouldering lump of charcoal. If it burned, he felt no pain. Slipping cautiously into the hatchway, he found the powder barrels. They had been closed and covered with a tarpaulin. Mindful of the revolving ball of twine in one hand, the lump of charcoal in the other, he was hard put to remove the coverings. But he accomplished it. Then he took a bit of greasy rope from his pocket, placed one end in the powder and stretched out the other end under the lump of charcoal. Softly, deliberately he blew upon it. The coal glowed pink, red, white. It was beautiful; it was alive; it smiled. Slowly the fuse ignited, sputtered, burst into flame.

Like a tiger he leaped upon the deck and dove into the sea.

Down into the cool depths! He swam under water far from the ship. A wave lifted him as if he had been a leaf. The white sails loomed over him and passed. The dark hull passed. The glow of the compass-light passed, and dark circle of still faces and red caps like spots of blood. The tide bore him on. Jaurez lost sight of the ship as he sank in the hollow of a wave, and found her again as he rose on a crest. Moments rolled on, lengthened out, wore into eternities! Would the flame never reach the powder? Had the rope burned out? Had he bungled? The saints save Campeche!

The great waves came one in seven.[4] He felt the gathering impetus of a huge swell. Forward he was flung—forward and up—up—up. There the ship rode, silver sails, vague black hull, faint circle of light. It was then a violent wind puffed in his face. An intense steel-blue blinding flash flared over the sea. And then followed sodden thunder.

Again a seventh wave hurled him aloft, as if in glory of its task, and showed him a confused mass, billowy like breakers, and spouts of fire. Then the black sharp bow of the ship pointed to the stars, poised for an instant, and slipped into the sea.

The cord drawing through his fingers reminded Jaurez of the girl. Swimming with swift powerful strokes he kept an easy hold of the line. Presently he was struck by the fact that there was no strain on the line; it appeared to sag and drift. He pulled it, and it slid readily to him. A fear beset him that it had broken. Suddenly he had the end in his hand; he felt the noose that he had fastened over the girl's wrist. It had slipped. He had lost her. She was gone. She was drifting on the sea.

Frantically he swam to and fro and around, and raised himself high on the waves to peer down into the hollows. There was no dark object on the pale glancing light of the water. He called. A low strange cry seemed to come to him. He swam toward it and called again. The cry mocked him from behind. It was only a sound of the sea. Then he faced the stars that he knew and swam steadily. The water was fresh and cool; the current hurried him onward. He thought of the long miles to the beach, of the yellow saw-toothed sharks, but felt no fear. He sorrowed for the girl he might have saved, and he had no hope. Before she could reach shore, the tide would ebb and would be too strong for her.

The Southern Cross drew a straight course for Jaurez. He swam easily, husbanding his strength, floating on the more violent waves, breasting the backlash. The heavens quickened and lightened with the rising of the moon. Like a molten world of shimmering opal the restless sea quivered under the radiant light. Something black shadowed the silver fire of a great swell. Jaurez lunged forward with his powerful stroke. He was caught on a seventh wave, swung aloft, and there on the crest in the white light he saw the girl.

"Oh! the saints be praised!" he cried.

Ollone was riding high, upheld by the cork jacket, and swimming with a slow measured stroke that told Jaurez she was used to the sea.

---

[4]Waves do vary in size and energy, but it is an old myth which says that every seventh wave is more powerful than the other six.

Jaurez, losing sight of her, floated on the waves and waited the next mighty swell that came one in seven. Long before it got to him, he felt the strange disturbance of the sea, a quivering, a response to some far driving force. He saw a slow dark upheaval, a starlit wall of water coming on. As he sank into a hollow the wave boomed over him, a glancing incline, with dimpling spin-drift crest. Up and up he was lifted in its long roll. He seemed flung to the stars. He saw Ollone. She, too, had been flung aloft. Then the great seventh wave flung the girl into his arms. It was as if the sea had given her to him. He supported her and spoke a word of cheer. She smiled. Was it the light of the moon which gave her that flash of life? How white her face!

He shortened his stroke so that she might keep even with him, and close together they swam with the tide. Once he asked her if her people had gone down with the *Metista* and she gave a sad affirmative. Then from time to time he spoke words of encouragement, always adding that Campeche was not far, that soon they would hear the boom of the surf. The moon climbed high and the night became a white night on a white sea. Slower he had to swim that he might not pass her. And from the top of every swell he scanned the horizon line, straining his eyes to see the white wall of Campeche, straining his ears to hear the boom of the surf.

The girl swam slower and slower till her strength failed and she rolled wearily. Jaurez turned her on her back, drew her against his breast and clasped her fast cramping hand round his neck. Then his strokes swept out restrained, measured and strong. He felt that he could swim forever. She floated under him so lightly that he had no sense of being burdened; at every stroke her body drifting upward touched his, breast to breast. Her white face rested low in the water and her hair splashed soft and silkily against his cheek. She watched him with wonderful eyes, dark like the hollows in the shadows of the swells.

The witchery of the sea was in Jaurez's blood. Suddenly the girl was as beautiful to him, as impelling; and like the tide which bore him shoreward was the birth and the rush and the might of his love.

"Ollone, I shall save you. It's in me to save you. For I love you. And I want to tell you while we are here—alone—on the sea—where love came to me. Will you love me—some day?"

"I love you now," she whispered.

He kissed her sweet wet lips, and above him whirled the star-sown sky.

Then he swam on through the opaque night—and on and on. And his motion slowed; the cold crept up his limbs; the cramp stiffened his arms. He drifted. He heard mocking roars and deep-toned knells from the depths. A shadow hovered over him. Lower he sank in the water—slower he drifted—more and more he wanted to sleep—farther away and dimmer grew the stars.

A faint new sound on the breeze rallied his deadening senses.

Boom!—long, low, lengthening roar—boom!

"Surf! Surf," he whispered. "Ollone! . . . . hear! the surf!"

Irresistible life came back to him. He heard the surf pounding the beach. Had he not lived his life with that deep sound in his ears? Boom! No lying trick of the brain—no hollow haunting roar of wind!—Boom! How he loved it, and the great waves, so helpful, so true! They had cast him up from the dark mystic moving sea. He saw Ollone's white face and closed eyes and sweet lips. He felt her hands locked cold around his neck.

The billows rising higher, raced with him on their curdled bosoms. Seaweed whipped his cheeks; sand stung in the flying spray. He heard a sound that was like a piercing blade of joy in his breast—the long withdrawing scream of the pebbles on the beach. Over the tumbling breakers he saw the high white wall of Campeche. Then it was as if the wonderful sea rose under him in its last and mightiest seventh wave. He was carried on the slope, cradled on its crest, hurried toward the curling white-frothed break, and hurled up the shore. But that seventh wave, selfish at the last and true to the sea, sullenly dragged and sucked at the girl in his arms. Jaurez fiercely resisted the wave, and slowly it receded with reluctant roar. Then he crawled up with the creeping foam and laid Ollone on the strand. A darkness mantled the white wall and the watch stars and the unquiet sea.

"TRAILS OVER THE GLASS MOUNTAINS"

Introduction

It is inevitable that people contradict themselves and that a man like Zane Grey, who railed at what the fledgling American tourist industry was doing to his beloved wilderness, should at the same time be the foremost wilderness tourist of his day. Zane Grey not only helped put northern Arizona and southern Utah on the visitor maps by compulsively writing about the desolate beauty of this region, he took film producer Jesse L. Lasky to Monument Valley and encouraged him to use the area for western movie settings, thereby guaranteeing that the region would become a scenic cliché.

From the time of his first writing success, Zane Grey became intrigued with the idea of converting his western romances into film. In 1919, he formed his own motion picture company but eventually sold the operation to Jesse Lasky who had made *The Squaw Man*, the first movie ever produced in Hollywood. Lasky took in a partner, Adolph Zukor, and the two men bought the old Brunton Studio where Zane Grey had his film company but changed the name to Paramount. This now famous studio is still in its same location.

Lasky and Zukor were grateful to Grey and in the years after were always generous to him in the terms with which they leased and re-leased his novels for the screen. Randolph Scott got his start playing Zane Grey's *Man of the Forest*, and even before Shirley Temple appeared in *Little Miss Marker*, she had played a rancher's daughter in Paramount's remake of *To The Last Man*. The list of other stars who got their start in Zane Grey's Paramount films include Richard Arlen, Jean Arthur, Wallace Beery, Harry Carey, Gary Cooper, Buster Crabbe, Jack Holt, Jack LaRue, William Powell, and Fay Wray.

During these years, Zane Grey borrowed some of the excellent cameramen Paramount developed and took them on trips so he would have film records of his angling explorations in such remote areas as Tahiti and New Zealand. The footage of leaping mako sharks and giant marlin was spectacular, and producer Sol Lesser, best known as the man who brought Tarzan to the screen, thought that despite the specialized subject matter, Zane Grey's "home movies" would have great commercial appeal. No one in Hollywood was interested, so Lesser took his feature-length *Zane Grey's South Sea Adventures* to New York City, rented a theater on West 42nd Street, and watched the money flow in. Within fourteen weeks, Lesser had recouped his investment, and the film was pure profit for over two years.

In 1971, while working on a book honoring the centennial of Zane Grey's birth in 1872, I visited ZG's son Romer in Altadena, California, and found his house filled with reels of old silver nitrate-based films dating back to 1919, when his father had started Zane Grey Productions. Lots of leaping fish were in the later movies, but the films had historical significance in what else they showed, including a spectrum of once-significant people long since dead and an American and South Pacific landscape long since altered. Romer knew the film was fading and becoming too brittle for projection, and he begged me to find some way to raise money to save the film, for we both knew that many old newsreels had been reprocessed and saved through one or another cultural grants.

I took the question to my friend and TV-movie producer Dale Bell who was working for the American Broadcasting Company at the time and is now associated with National Geographic television specials. Dale asked around the television industry, and we were both surprised when we got a very enthusiastic call to come in and talk about the possibility of a Zane Grey special with the William Morris Agency. Although I didn't see how a talent agency would fit into the preservation of historical films, I went to the meeting with high hopes.

What we found was a ludicrous parody of how talent agencies work. The executives all wore open-collared, flowery-patterned shirts and sandals, called each other "sweetheart" and "pussycat," and patronized us tie-wearing squares. Their plan was to use the name of Zane Grey as a peg on which to hang a series of cameo appearances by a good many of the agency's old and, in some cases, nearly forgotten actors and actresses. It didn't even matter whether these stars had actually gotten their starts in Zane Grey westerns; so long as William Morris owned them, they would say they began with Zane Grey.

"What difference does it make?" asked one of the pussycats. "What difference does it make?"

Guide John Wetherill (left), Zane Grey, and movie producer Jesse Lasky pause after crossing the Glass Mountains on their way to Rainbow Bridge several years after the trip described in the following story.

"Now, sweethearts, the way we'll open is to have Randy Scott ride up out of Monument Valley, stop in front of the camera and start talking about the time Zane Grey took him and a Paramount crew into the valley."

"But Zane Grey never did that."

"What difference does it make?"

"After the beer commercial"—the subordinate pussycats tittered—"we'll have Tony Perkins at Rainbow Bridge remembering his first Zane Grey movie."

"But Perkins was never in a Zane Grey movie!"

"What difference does it make?"

"Will you be able to salvage any of the footage owned by Romer Grey?" I asked.

"Maybe a couple of shots of his father on horseback," the chief pussycat said. "Most of the rest shows Zane Grey setting off to kill poor creatures that never did anyone any harm, and we certainly don't want to show that to family audiences, do we?"

"But you are willing to make up a pack of lies about the origins of the film industry!"

"What difference does it make?"

Dale and I got up to leave. The pussycats followed, meowing that we were making a terrible mistake. I don't think we did. True, Romer Grey is now dead, and the film he had is in even sorrier shape then it was a dozen years ago. But the memory of the desert country that Zane Grey loved, and of the animals he used to traverse it is more honestly alive in stories like "Trails Over the Glass Mountains," first published in the January 1924 issue of *Outdoor America*, than it would have been in any pussycat presentation.

GWR

TRAILS OVER THE
GLASS MOUNTAINS

In 1913 John Wetherill,[1] noted scout and Indian trader of northern Arizona, took me to the wonderful Rainbow Bridge. We rode and climbed some of the hardest trails in the southwest, and in so doing suffered the loss of several horses—a heart-breaking experience. Most of these misadventures befell us in cross a range of low mountains of smooth polished wind-worn rock that we named the Glass Mountains.

In April, 1922, I undertook the same journey, taking as trail comrades my brother, R. C., and my friend Wiborn. Wetherill, with his Indians and cowboys, had charge of the guiding and packing; and Lee Doyle, son of the old pioneer, Al Doyle,[2] who had been my guide for ten years, had charge of my own horses.

Wetherill strongly advised against taking these horses; and he was wholly sincere in his argument as to the risks. All the horses I have written about, except Silvermane and Wildfire, both wild stallions of the uplands, I have owned. Night, the beautiful charger who raced with Black Star in *Riders of the Purple Sage*, is still living and as noble and spirited and beautiful as ever. Of course I would never risk him on bad trails. He has earned his rest in green pastures and clear waters, where he can graze and whistle and prance and drink to his heart's content. Especially loth was Wetherill to endanger our five favorites—White

---

[1] The brothers John and Richard Wetherill settled in Arizona in the 1890s, and popular magazine articles by Richard is what first attracted other white people to this part of the country.
[2] The Doyles and Ben and Ed Haught were Zane Grey's guides and hunting companions when he pursued deer, turkey, bear and mountain lion in the Grand Canyon and on the Kaibab Plateau.

Stockings, Sarchedon, Cricket, Nig, and Mary Mullen. It would have been pretty hard to beat any of them.[3]

White Stockings was my favorite, a superb bay with white face and white feet. He was spirited, intelligent, and had the easiest gait of any horse I ever bestrode. To ride him was like sitting in a rocking-chair. He was practically tireless. A remarkable feature about White Stockings was the fact that he was built so that a saddle never slipped on him, even on the steepest trails. He could run like a streak. I had tested out all these good points during three fall hunting trips over the rough timbered country of the Tonto Basin.

Sarchedon was a big dark charger of a horse, hard to manage and ride, but the kind that cowboys chose—which is the best praise of any horse. He had been with us on four trips. Cricket was a yellow bay, rather small in stature, but well built, and a graceful stepper. He had an easy trot, and he would get out in front of the outfit and stay there all day. If any horse passed him, he would be restless and fretful until he got the lead again. Cricket did not like cowboys. He had belonged to Lee Doyle's sister who had ridden him when she was a child and he was a colt; and perhaps that was why he did his best work for a woman rider. But in his eight previous trips with me, he had thoroughly proved his value. Nig was a coal black horse, not particularly remarkable for points. He did not show off. Apparently he was lazy, sleepy. But Lee Doyle declared him the safest horse, the best horse on bad trails that he had ever had any experience with. Nig had chased lions and bears, and kept with the hounds on many of our hunts in the Tonto, and he had a reputation second to none. Mary Mullen was a beautiful racer, a dark clean-cut slender horse, young, spirited, rather wild, and as Lee put it, sometimes in too big a hurry on bad trails.

In spite of Wetherill's solicitous fears, Lee advised me to take my own horses, risk or no risk. They had been eating grain and alfafa for two months and were in perfect condition. The Indian mustangs Wetherill used had just been rounded up from a desert range where grass had been scarce that winter. They were not in good shape, and Wetherill admitted

---

[3]Although Zane Grey was 35 years old when he made his first trip to that area of the West which made him rich and he made famous, he did his homework on everything pertaining to western traditions so well that he soon knew far more about the region than any of the critics who pooh-poohed him for not being a native son. Although all Westerners assume they intuitively know everything that needs to be known about horses, most don't even know how to ride well. Zane Grey did, supremely well, and the following paragraphs reveal a marvellous understanding of equine temperament. His daughter, Betty Zane, shared her father's love of horses, and when she came of marrying age, it was the natural choice for her to turn her back on more cosmopolitan alternatives and to choose a California rancher.

it. He said each of us could ride one until it gave out and then take another.

So I was rather in a quandry. What decided me in the end to take my own horses was the fact that R. C. and Wiborn had both suffered exceedingly on the long desert ride from Flagstaff to Kayenta. R. C. had started out with a crippled shoulder and should never have come at all. Wiborn's bad legs, overworked in his college athletic days when he was champion of the track team, had buckled under him. Moreover, we had encountered snow, sleet, icy gales, sand and dust storms, and hot weather, all in that ten days' ride out to Wetherill's. We not only needed, but deserved the best of horses. Whereupon I decided the matter.

"Wetherill, we'll take my own horses," I said. "Put R. C. on Nig. Lee will ride Sarch. I'll ride Stockings. And we'll let Wiborn start out on that great mule of yours."

"I wish I had one like him for all of us to ride," observed the trader.

"Why a mule for me?" demanded my friend, loftily. "I can ride Mary Mullen."

"I reckon you could—for a way," I replied. "But wait till we get over to the Glass Mountains."

Both my brother and friend, new to this upland country, inquired rather dubiously and concernedly about these Glass Mountains. I looked at Wetherill, and he explained that the hills mentioned were some steep slippery slopes of rock where he always lost horses.

"Humph!" commented my crippled brother.

Wiborn's hazel eyes shadowed with a far-off expression of longing, as if he had suddenly thought of home.

"Wetherill, you once told me about an old Piute trail that led over the Navajo Mountain," I said. "Have you ever taken anyone on it?"

"No. I started out with a fellow some years back, but he only lasted one day."

"Then there haven't been any white men on this Piute trail?"

"Shore I reckon not," he drawled.

"Well," said I grimly, "it's your Piute trail for us—then the Glass Mountains—and then the Rainbow Trail and Nonnezoshe[4]—all in one trip."

"Now you're talking," declared Wetherill.

R. C. uttered a faint groan and sagged back against a bale of wool. Wiborn seemed bereft of that usual radiance characteristic of him.

---

[4] Modern publications spell this *Nonnezoshi*, meaning in Navajo, "the rainbow turned to stone," Rainbow Bridge.

"Never said I'd come on this trip," he declared. "Never said it!"

"Well, you've both come so far, and you're going to finish," I replied. "When we get down in the canyons out of the cold you fellows will warm up. Don't lose your enthusiasm just because there are no bear or turkey or fish on this trip. It is certainly the most beautiful trail in the west and worth all the hardship."

This narrative is concerned with the Glass Mountains. What our experience was on Wetherill's Piute trail shall be chronicled elsewhere. Suffice it to say here that our genial guide ran true to western form, inasmuch as he had not represented Piute trail half so heart-breaking as it turned out to be.

From the slope of Navajo Mountain, where the long cedar and piñon bench broke off abruptly and looked down into the vast naked Utah wilderness, there is a scene unparalleled in the west.

It fell to me to name it Marching Rocks. From east and north for over a hundred miles a wild world of windworn rocks waved and piled toward us. It bore some semblance to a stupendous flock of gray and yellow sheep with round backs closely pressed together. But every one of these bare stone backs was almost a mountain in itself, and surely in between each one was a crevice that was in reality a deep canyon. Piute Canyon was there, and Escalante Canyon, and San Juan Canyon, and the Grand Canyon—all mere winding dark threads across the leagues of stone. In the foreground the mass broke into stragglers, as if the leaders of the flock were marching ahead. How singularly did the effect of life, of action, strike the eye!

Away beneath us to the west yawned a green rolling plain of cedar across which ran the range of glassy stone hills we had to climb. They looked close, yet were perhaps twenty miles distant. Beyond seemed to spread a chaos of red and yellow walls, ramparts, crags, towers, and bewildering expanse of tilted earth, bare as bleached ribs of bone, extending far as the eye could see. One striking landmark dominated the scene—Wild Horse Mesa—a stupendous red-walled mountain, frowning, black-fringed and isolated. Insurmountable as it seemed, I vowed to climb it some day.[5] It was well to gaze at this wind-worn wilderness from so far aloft, for once down there, a true perspective was not possible.

We camped that night under the huge looming bulk of Navajo Mountain, on one of the beautiful cedar and sage upland plains I love so well. The purple sage spread on all sides, fragrant, colorful, strangest and

---

[5] He did better than climb it. Some years after this trip, in 1928, he published a novel entitled *Wild Horse Mesa*.

most beautiful growth of the desert. Piute Indians visited us. We saw the remarkable mustangs of this remnant of a once large tribe. Some were buckskin white with black mane reaching the sage, and with longer tail just as black. The Indians left us when darkness fell. At night the sweetness and loneliness and silence of this upland was beyond words to describe.

Next day, early in the afternoon, we reached the base of our Mountains of Glass. At this point the beauty of scenery no longer appealed to me. True, I experienced a keen thrill, but it was one of the cold species, rather chilling to the marrow. Wetherill dismounted and came over to me.

"Reckon you remember how we've got to keep on the move," he warned. "I'll go ahead with the boys and the pack mules. And I'll snap a picture when the chance offers. Lee had better hang back with you, in case you might need help. If a horse slips get out of his way, that's all."

The necessity for keeping in action here on these smooth slopes had always made it difficult to get good pictures of horses and men in the most dangerous places. But this time we had five cameras and expected results.

"Now the idea is this," I suggested. "When one of us gets in a safe place he can snap a picture of the other fellow in a bad place."

Wetherill led the way, climbing as rapidly as possible up the first steep incline. The pack train of mules followed him, and it was remarkable to see how precisely they kept in line with him. There really was no trail. When half a dozen of those laden mules became silhouetted on the sky-line they made a thrilling sight.

I sent my companions ahead, with Lee in the lead, and I took the rear, leading Stockings and holding my camera in readiness. Steep as was this slope, it was easy to climb because of the soft sandstone. The shoes of the horses and the hobnails in our boots cut deep enough to make slipping unlikely. But in my case the ascent was rendered uncomfortable because Stockings climbed so fast. I could not make him slow up. Therefore I had to stay ahead of him. He kept bumping me with his head, and twice he stepped on my heels, once hurting me considerably.

When we got on top, the pack train was out of sight. The bare summits of this glassy range resemble the surface of a heaving sea. I was out of breath. We all rested a moment. Stockings knew this was an unusual procedure. He was not excited or scared. But I thought he seemed rather nervous and in somewhat of a hurry to get the business over.

R. C.'s horse, for all the concern he showed, might have been climbing such trails all his life. Cricket lived up to his repute. But Lee had trouble with Mary Mullen. He had strapped a pack of bedding round Mary and

Zane Grey and guide Lee Doyle pose with a pair of black bears killed on a hunting trip to the Tonto Basin in northern Arizona. ZG rated Doyle and his father as among the most savvy horsemen he ever met in the West.

perhaps that annoyed her. Anyway Lee could not lead both Sarchedon and Mary, and so he let Mary go on.

"She'll knock a mule over sure," he said. "Maybe I'd better ride up these slopes, anyway."

"Don't do it," I said.

But Lee was still a cowboy and bad slopes meant nothing to him. Mounting Sarch he rode on over the summit and down out of sight. Here Wiborn's mule answered to the instincts of his kind, and while Wiborn was snapping a picture he trotted on after the other mules.

We went on to the brow of the hill and suddenly came in sight of the pack train winding round a curve lower down. The mules had gotten ahead of Wetherill. For a moment I lost myself in gazing at the wild strange scene. Then I remembered my camera. Of course we could have rested there as long as we cared to, but the plan was to keep in sight of the others for the sake of possible pictures.

We started after Lee. Wiborn now had no horse to bother him, so he was free to use his camera at will. R. C. seemed perfectly confident of Nig, and I concluded he had every reason to be. Stockings, however, was a different proposition. I followed in the rear of the others. Starting down the rather steep incline I held my bridle out at right angles, and called Stockings to come. Without hesitation he followed me, but instead of paying any attention to the bridle he kept at my heels. I saw at once that my walking gave him confidence. Where I walked he could certainly go. He did not mind this in the least. But he would not follow me slowly. I had to go fast, and I could not keep from being directly in front of him. The peril to me lay in the possibility of his slipping and knocking me down the slope. But as there was no precipice on this particular hill the danger was not great.

Once down off this summit I drew a deep breath of relief and fortified myself for what lay ahead. After I had threaded my way in and out and around a maze of curves, corners, and slopes, I came abruptly upon the others. It was not a bad place, but a sort of bowl in the hills. The outfit was scattered along the depression, and in the middle somebody was having trouble. I hurried on, and when I got where I could see, I was much concerned. Wetherill was running down towards a cowboy below. This individual was holding to a mule that appeared in danger of sliding over.

"Assistance! Assistance!" yelled this cowboy. His use of the word inclined me to the opinion that he was in fun, but his voice was convincing enough. Nevertheless we laughed. Wetherill reached him and together they held the mule until the other boys got there. When the mule was rescued from his precarious position and the cavalcade had straightened out, I asked Lee what had happened.

"Mary Mullen tried to force her way past that mule and knocked him off the trail," replied Lee. "The mule fell and turned clear over twice.

How he ever escaped sliding over the cliff I can't understand. Wetherill said goodbye to that mule and so did I."

We went on, somewhat sobered by this incident. And as we climbed and descended and wound our way onward, the conformation and substance of the rock hills changed. The slopes led down more steeply to abrupt precipices; and the soft sandstone gave way to something nearly as hard as granite. It was easy for a horse to slip, and they all slipped here and there. But for a horse to slip with one foot was not particularly serious. It was when he slipped with both front feet at once, or one front and one hind foot that he was in danger.

At last we came to what Wetherill considered the worst turn of the trail. Here he had lost most horses and mules. It was a narrow foot-wide trail round a corner projecting over an abyss. The rock was hard as flint, and the width of this trail slanted perceptibly toward the precipice. The instant I saw the place again I regretted that I had subjected my horses to such risks. Here there was little danger for a man, so long as he kept free of his horse. I watched the pack mules creep cautiously round the bend and pass out of sight. Wetherill yelled for me to wait to be the last. Wiborn remained behind with me, intending to photograph me crossing the bad place.

Here Stockings grew restive and pounded the hard rock with his hoofs. I tried to calm him. But he tossed his head and snorted. There was fire in his eye. And I grew alarmed.

Lee, who stood across the declivity with Wetherill, yelled to me. "Come on quick. Stockings thinks he's being left behind. Don't wait. He'll make it like a breeze. Only hurry."

Thus admonished I started down the little bowl-shaped depression that led to the narrow trail. Stockings was too eager. He slipped with all four feet and fell on his side. I held to the bridle, but I was suddenly paralyzed with fear for him. Stockings slid a yard or so, then luckily stopped on the last level of this bowl.

"Pull him up!" yelled Lee. "Talk to him! And come on!"

I did as I was bidden, and it seemed that I was more frightened than my horse. Once on his feet, he shook all over and he snorted. His fine dark eyes seemed to take me in, and the abyss and his narrow escape and the trail ahead. He knew. And at the moment I believed a great deal depended on me. I rose to the occasion.

"Come on, Stockings," I called, and climbed up the slight slope and walked out on the narrow trail as if it was no different from any other place. I saw only the white nicks in the hard stone made by the iron shoes of the other horses. I did not look up or to right or left. Yet I seemed to see

The goal of ZG's trips over the Glass Mountains was Rainbow Bridge. A remote National Monument in the 1920s, the great stone arch was made easily accessible to boaters in the late 1960s by the drowned Colorado River backed up behind Glen Canyon Dam.

that deep yawning gulf at my side. I heard Stockings pounding close at my heels. I did not feel any strain on the bridle. I walked as fast as I could to keep ahead of him. What an endless time before I bumped into Wetherill and found myself on level ground!

"By Golly! that was a close shave for him," exclaimed the trader, with relief. "I'll say he acted fine."

"Stockings did not want to be left behind," said Lee.

"Whew! I'm glad that's past. . . . . But we have to come back!" I replied, finding a place to sit down and compose myself. I was wet with cold sweat and had a constriction in my throat. To have seen Stockings slide over the cliff would have been terrible. As for him, the incident was past. He whistled for the other horses and pawed the rock impatiently.

We went on and had a long respite from chills up our backs until we came to the descent on the far side of the Glass Mountains. This I knew would be an ordeal. The slope was steep and smooth, almost as polished as marble. Wetherill had cut nicks in the rock in the zigzag trail that led down. We watched the pack-mules start down with the Indian in the lead. In a few moments they were out of sight.

"I'll lead with Sarch," said Lee to me. "You come next, with Nig behind. That'll steady Stockings. I'm sure glad Mary Mullen is down."

We started about fifty feet apart. To my mind, in view of the years of experience I have had since my first passage over these mountains, no fine and spirited horse should ever be put to such trails, unless on a mission of vital importance. I was thrilled and ashamed at once.

This was a long slope that had to be zigzagged down with neither haste nor pause. Stockings followed me precisely as before, no slower nor faster. Sometimes I had to slide to keep out of his way. But I kept his hoofs on the nicked trail in the hard rocks. Sometimes I walked sidewise, looking back at him. He would step so that only the up slope side of his shoes touched the rock. He could not place his hoofs on a level. There was no level. But so far as I could see he did not show the slightest fear. I grew certain that my walking ahead of him made him feel safe. As a matter of fact he was in great peril. If he had slipped as before he would have slid half a thousand feet to his death.

Experiences like this prove what intelligence and courage horses have. Like dogs they are the friends and helpers of man. If I had not treasured White Stockings before this time, I certainly would have done so now. He might just as well have balked on that treacherous slope. But because I bade him follow and talked to him and led him, he came willingly, eagerly, for that time at least, dependent upon me.

Step by step, close together, we made the long crooked descent without

a single slip. When I edged off the last steep slant of rock I was surprised to find all the others waiting for me. R. C. with Nig had made a boulevard of that descent. They had passed me without my knowing.

"Fine and dandy," declared Wetherill, in hearty relief. "Shore they're some horses! It's much safer going home, because the bad places are mostly up hill."

R. C. had evidently been stirred by this successful and thrilling conquest of the range of slippery hills.

"Lead me to your Wild Horse Mesa," he said, dauntlessly. "I'll ride Nig up that."

Wiborn looked around for the mule which had deserted him.

"You long-eared ass of antiquity!" he retorted. "You put one over on me, huh? Well, I was tickled to death to lose you. And I got here first!"

After a rest we mounted and rode on, happy that the danger to horses was past for the present, and glad once more to be free to look ahead at the winding cedared valley and up at the lofty walls. We were to camp in Surprise Valley,[6] that wonderful canyoned maze. And as we worked down deeper the air grew warm and still, the colored walls lifted higher. Indian primrose and paintbrush bloomed under the cedars. Running water made music under the silent walls. Sunset was gilding the towering crags when we climbed to the one portal of Surprise Valley and gazed down into this marvelous niche of solitude and beauty. Wind-sculptured towering walls of red and gold! And far above them, and far away, loomed Wild Horse Mesa, shrouded in the lilac haze of sunset, calling me, bidding me sometime to surmount it. In this strange desert country there was always a larger experience. Not enough had been conquest of the Piute Trail and the Mountains of Glass! Wild Horse Mesa presented a sterner obstacle. To toil, to endure, to seek, to find, and not to yield— that was the lesson of the desert.

---

[6]This is the same Surprise Valley in *Riders of the Purple Sage* where Lassiter, the old Texas Ranger and gunfighter, his niece Fay, and Jane Withersteen make their stand against their Mormon persecutors and crush them, but trap themselves forever inside this earthly paradise by rolling an enormous but delicately balanced boulder into the only passage in or out of the valley.

"MONTY PRICE'S NIGHTINGALE"

Introduction

Every successful Victorian writer believed that no story should be told unless it had a moral. In addition, every tale should have at least one shining act of virtue from which the reader could possibly pattern a moment in his own life. In this way, each Victorian writer believed he or she was not only making a unique contribution to literature, but further- ing mankind (meaning the middle to upper classes of Europe and the Americas) in our rise toward human perfection. Not for the Victorians would have been the funny and thoughtful remark of William Faulkner that had he not written Faulkner, somebody else would have.

Temperamentally, even if not historically, Zane Grey was a Victorian. He believed in the perfectability of mankind, at least Anglo-Saxons like himself,[1] and he wrote for moral purposes as much as he wrote for money. Yet he modernized the nineteenth century good-guy struggle with the bad-guy by making his good guys partly bad, and his bad guys sometimes good. This was considered to be pretty subtle stuff for the pulp markets of the 1910s and 1920s, but Zane Grey never thought of himself as subtle. Indeed, he might have objected to the word, insisting that both he and his work were "straight forward."

ZG achieved a certain depth even in his gun-fighters and villains by mixing one or more elements of his own personality in every major character he created. He knew that all people are made up of good and

---

[1] Writing for *Outdoor America*, ZG observed "When . . . George Washington made his farewell speech, the population of his beloved America was 87.5 percent Anglo-Saxon. In this year of Our Lord, 1924, that Anglo-Saxon strength has gone down to 53 percent. And that percent is practicing race suicide. I place Anglo-Saxon blood, America, and love of forests—love of freedom, inseparable."

Zane Grey was no more (or less) familar with horses than most
other men of his generation when he made his first trip West at
age 35. Yet because he was a wonderful natural athlete and a
man of great will, he soon became one of the best horsemen in
Arizona and California. On more than one occasion when
someone was needed to handle a panicky horse on a movie set
or at a crowded railway station, ZG became the man of the
hour.

bad qualities, and he was a craftsman at developing credible crises in which some people under stress performed nobly, while others thought only of themselves.

Although Zane Grey was never a drinker, drug user, nor a smoker, he was tempted by some of the young women who fluttered around him, seeking employment as his secretary, his children's nanny, or any other way they might remain near his radiant fame. Zane Grey loved his wife and felt remorse for the lust within his heart and his rare lapses of infidelity. But remorse was not enough for this Victorian writer. He converted his experience and emotion into the best kind of moralistic fiction.

The following story poses a dilemma for its hero—who, when the story opens, is no hero at all. Does Monty Price yield to his base instincts and respond to the siren call of the woman with "the dark, mocking, luring eyes?" Or does he do what must be done? This superb yarn appeared in the April 1924 issue of *Outdoor America*.

GWR

MONTY PRICE'S
NIGHTINGALE

Round the camp fires they cursed him in hearty cowboy fashion, and laid upon him the ban of their ill will. They said that Monty Price had no friend—that no foreman or rancher ever trusted him—that he never spent a dollar—that he would not keep a job—that there must be something crooked about a fellow who bunked and worked alone, who quit every few months to ride away, no one knew where, and who returned to the ranges, haggard and thin and shaky, hunting for another place.

He had been drunk somewhere, and the wonder of it was that no one in the Tonto Forest Ranges had ever seen him drink a drop. Red Lake and Gallatin and Bellville knew him, but no more of him than the ranges. He went farther afield, they said, and hinted darker things than a fling at a faro or a fondness for red liquor.

But there was no rancher, no cowboy from one end of the vast range country to another who did not admit Monty Price's preeminence in those peculiar attributes of his calling. He was a magnificent rider; he had an iron and cruel hand with a horse, yet he never killed or crippled his mount; he possessed the Indian instinct for direction; he never failed on the trail of lost stock; he could ride an outlaw and brand a wild steer and shoe a vicious mustang as bragging cowboys swore they could; and supreme test of all, he would endure, without complaint, long toilsome hours in the piercing wind and freezing sleet and blistering sun.

"I'll tell you what," said old Abe Somers. "I've ranched from the Little Big Horn to the Pecos, an' I've seen a sight of cowpunchers in my day. But Monty Price's got 'em all skinned. It shore is too bad he's onreliable packin' off the way he does, jest when he's the boy most needed. Some mystery about Monty."

It was an old story in the Tonto—how once when Monty returned from one of his strange absences and rode in to Cass Stringer's.

Cass was the biggest rancher in those parts, and, as it happened, at the time was without a foreman and in urgent need of men. "Monty, I'll give you a job—make you foreman—double any wages you ever got—if you'll promise to stick through summer and the fall round-up." Monty made the promise, and he ran Cass' outfit as it had never been run before; and then, with the very day of the round-up at hand, he broke his word and rode away.

That hurt Monty in the Tonto country. He never got another foreman job, but it seemed he could always find some outfit that would employ him. And strangely he was always at one and the same time unwelcome and welcome. His record made him unpopular. But, on the other hand, while he was with an outfit, he made for efficiency and speed. The extra duty, the hard task, the problem with stock or tools or harness—these always fell to Monty. His most famous trick was to offer to take a comrade's night shift.

So it often happened that while the cowboys lolled round their camp fire, Monty Price, after a hard day's riding, would stand out the night guard, in rain and snow. But he always made a bargain. He sold his service. And the boys were wont to say that he put his services high. Still they would never have grumbled at that if Monty had ever spent a dollar. He saved his money. He never bought any fancy boots or spurs or bridles or scarfs or chaps; and his cheap jeans and saddles were the jest of his companions.

Nevertheless, in spite of Monty's shortcomings, he rode in the Tonto on and off for five years before he made an enemy.

There was a cowboy named Bart Muncie who had risen to be a foreman and who eventually went to ranching on a small scale. He acquired a range up in the forest country where grassy valleys and parks lay between the wooded hills, and here in a wild spot among the pines he built a cabin for his wife and baby. It came about that Monty went to work for Muncie, and rode for him for six months. Then, in a dry season, with Muncie short of help and with long drives to make, Monty quit in his inexplicable way and left the rancher in dire need. Muncie lost a good deal of stock that fall, and he always blamed Monty for it.

Some weeks later it chanced that Muncie was in Bellville the very day Monty returned from his latest mysterious absence. And the two met in a crowded store.

Monty appeared vastly different from the lean-jawed, keen-eyed, hard-riding cowboy of a month back. He was haggard and thin and shaky and spiritless and somber.

"See here, Monty Price," said Muncie with stinging scorn, "I reckon you'll spare me a minute of your precious time."

"I reckon so," replied Monty.

Muncie used up more than the alloted minute in calling Monty every bad name known to the range.

"An' the worst of all you are is thet you're a liar!" concluded the rancher passionately. "I relied on you an' you failed me. You lost me a herd of stock. Put me back a year! An' for what? God only knows what! We ain't got you figgered here—not thet way. But after this trick you turned me, we all know you're not square. An' I go on record callin' you as you deserve. You're no good. You've got a streak of yellow, an' you sneak off now an' then to indulge it. An' most of all you're a liar! Now, if it ain't all so—flash your gun!"

But Monty Price did not draw.

The scorn and abuse of the cowboys might never have been for all the effect it had on Monty. He did not see it or feel it. He found employment with a rancher named Wentworth, and went at this work in the old, inimitable manner that was at once the admiration and despair of his fellows. He rolled out of his blankets in the gray dawn, and he was the last to roll in at night. In a week all traces of his weakened condition had vanished, and he grew strong and dark and hard, once more like iron. And then again he was up to his old tricks, more intense than ever, eager and gruff at bargaining his time, obsessed by the one idea—to make money.

To Monty the long, hot dusty, blasting days of summer were as moments. Time flew for him. The odd jobs; the rough trails; the rides without water or food; the long stands in the cold rain; the electric storms when the lightning played around and crackled in his horse's mane, and the uneasy herd bawled and milled—all these things that were the everlasting torment of his comrades were as nothing to Monty. He endured the smart of rope-burned wrist, the bruise and chafe and ache of limb—all the knocks and hurts of this strenuous work, and he endured them as if they were not.

And when the first pay day came and Monty tucked away a little roll of greenbacks inside his vest, and kept adding to it as one by one his comrades paid him for some bargained service—then in Monty Price's heart began the low and insistent and sweetly alluring call of the thing that had ruined him. Thereafter sleeping or waking, he lived in a dream, with that music in his heart, and the hours were fleeting.

On the mountain trails, in the noonday heat of the dusty ranges, in the dark, sultry nights with their thunderous atmosphere he was always listening to that song of his nightingale. To his comrades he seemed a silent, morose, greedy cowboy, a demon for work, with no desire for friendship, no thought of home or kin, no love of a woman or a horse or anything, except money. To Monty himself, his whole inner life grew rosier and mellower and richer as day by day his nightingale sang sweeter and louder. Every time he felt that little bundle inside his vest, a warm and delicious thrill went over him. On the long rides he pressed it with his hand a hundred times to feel if it were there, to feel the substance that made possible the fulfillment of his dream. Like a slave he toiled to add to that precious treasure.

Deep planted in his soul was a passion that drove him, consumed him. It enormously magnified the importance of his little wage, of his bargaining with his fellows, of his jealous saving. It was the very life and fire of his blood—the bent of his mind—the secret of his endurance and his dream. And when he was away from the chuck wagon and the camp fire, out on the windy range or up in the pine-sloped forest, alone and free, then he was strangely happy, thoughtlessly happy, living in his dream, planning and waiting, always listening to the song of his nightingale.

And that song was a song of secret revel—far away—where he gave up to this wind of flame that burned within him—where a passionate and irresistible strain in his blood found its outlet—where wanton red lips whispered, and wanton eyes, wine dark and seductive, lured him, and wanton arms twined around him.

The rains failed to come that summer. The gramma grass bleached on the open ranges and turned yellow up in the parks. But there was plenty of grass and water to last out the fall. It was fire the ranchers feared.[2]

Up on the forest ridges snow was always due in November. But the driest fall ever known in the Tonto passed into winter without rain or snow. On the open prairie the white grass waved in the wind, so dry it crinkled; and the forest ridges were tinder boxes waiting for a spark. The ranchers had all their men riding up the parks and draws and slopes after the cattle that kept working farther and farther up. The stock that strayed was wild and hard to hold. There were far too few cowboys. And it was predicted, unless luck changed the weather, that there would be serious losses.

---

[2]And fire that Zane Grey feared and loathed. Writing in *Outdoor America* the month before this story appeared, ZG noted that "Mr. [William B.] Greeley [Chief of the U.S. Forest Service] reports 62,000 forest fires during 1923. Not sixty-two! Let me repeat! Sixty-two *thousand!* I venture to state from my own observation that 61,000 of them were the result of thoughtlessness, carelessness, ignorance and indifference on the part of persons who in the main have no love for the forests. In the sections of our forest land that I have visited during late years I have run across only one forest fire from lightning striking a dead tree, and hundreds of fires caused by cigarette smokers and careless campers."

One morning above the low, gray-stoned and black-fringed mountain range rose clouds of thick, creamy smoke. There was fire on the other side of the mountain. But unless the wind changed and drew fire in over the pass there was no danger on that score. The wind was right; it seldom changed at that season, though sometimes it blew a gale. Still the ranchers grew more anxious. The smoke clouds rolled up and spread and hid the top of the mountain, and then lifted slow, majestic columns of white and yellow toward the sky.

On the day that Wentworth, along with other alarmed ranchers, sent men up to fight the fire in the pass, Monty Price quit his job and rode away. He did not tell anybody. He just took his little pack and his horse, and in the confusion of the hour he rode away. For days he felt that his call might come at any moment, and finally it had come. It did not occur to him that he was quitting Wentworth at a most critical time; and it would not have made any difference to him if it had occurred to him.

He rode away with bells in his heart. He felt like a boy at the prospect of a wonderful adventure. He felt like a man who had toiled and slaved, whose ambition had been supreme, and who had reached the pinnacle where his longing would be gratified. His freedom stirred in him the ecstatic emotion of the shipwrecked mariner who from a lonely height beheld a sail. He was strained, tense, overwrought. For six months he had been chained to toil he hated. And now he was free. He was going. He was on the way. The keen wind seemed like wine. For once he saw the blue of the sky, the beauty of the bold peaks in the distance. And he pulled in his horse upon the ridge of a high foothill, where the trail forked, and looked across the ranges, away toward the south that called him.

Monty Price was still a young man. Of light and powerful build, rangy and wiry, darkly bronzed with eyes like coals of fire, he appeared a handsome cowboy. His face was hard set, stern, like that of all men of his kind, and there was nothing in it to suggest his failing or that he deserved the brand that Muncie had put upon him. He seemed good to look at. There was something of the open, free ranges in his look and his action.

The smell of burning pine turned Monty round to face the north. There was valley below him, then open slopes, and patches of pine, rising gently to billow darkly with the timbered mass of the mountain. A pall of smoke curled away from the crest, borne on a strong wind. The level line of smoke broke sharply at the pass and turned toward him, running down into the saddle between the bluffs. The fire in the pass was gaining. He thought grimly that all the men in the Tonto country could not check it.

"Sure she's goin' to burn over," he muttered. "An' if the wind changes—whoopee!"

His road led to the right, away from the higher ground and the timber. To his left the other road wound down the ridge to the valley below and stretched on through straggling pines and clumps of cedar toward the slopes and the forests. Monty had ridden that road a thousand times. For it led to Muncie's range. And as Monty's keen eye swept on over the parks and the thin wedge of pine to the black mass to timber beyond he saw something that made him draw up with a start. Clearly defined against the blue-black swelling slope was a white-and-yellow cloud of smoke. It was moving. At thirty miles distance, that it could be seen to move at all was proof of the great speed with which it was traveling.

"She's caught!" he exclaimed. "Way down on this side. An' she'll burn over. Nothin' can save the range!"

He watched, and those keen, practiced eyes made out the changing swelling columns of smoke, the widening path, the creeping dim red.

"Reckon that'll surprise Wentworth's outfit," soliloquized Monty thoughtfully. "It doesn't surprise me none. An' Muncie, too. His cabin's up there in the valley."

It struck Monty suddenly that the wind blew hard in his face. It was sweeping straight down the valley toward him. It was bringing that fire. Swift on the wind!

"One of them sudden changes of wind!" he said. "Veered right around! An' Muncie's range will go. An' his cabin!"

Straightway Monty grew darkly thoughtful. He had remembered seeing Muncie with Wentworth's men on the way to the pass. In fact, Muncie was the leader of this fire-fighting brigade.

"Sure he's fetched down his wife an' the baby," he muttered. "I didn't see them. But sure he must have."

Monty's sharp gaze sought the road for tracks. No fresh track showed! Muncie must have taken his family over the short-cut trail. Certainly he must have! Monty remembered Muncie's wife and child. The woman had hated him. But little Del with her dancing golden curls and her blue eyes—she had always had a ready smile for him. It came to Monty then suddenly, strangely, that little Del would have loved him if he had let her. Where was she now? Safe at Wentworth's without a doubt. But then she might not be. Muncie had certainly no fears of fire in the direction of home, not with the wind in the north and no prospect of change. It was quite possible—it was probable that the rancher had left his family at home that morning.

Monty experienced a singular shock. It had occurred to him to ride down to Muncie's cabin and see if the woman and child had been left. And whether or not he found them there the matter of getting back was a long chance. That wind was strong—that fire was sweeping down. How murky, red, sinister the slow-moving cloud!

"I ain't got a lot of time to decide," he said. His face turned pale and beads of sweat came out upon his brow.

That sweet little golden-haired Del, with her blue eyes and her wistful smile! Monty saw her as if she had been there. Then like lightning flashed back the thought that he was on his way to his revel. And the fires of hell burst in his veins. And more deadly sweet than any siren music rang the song of his nightingale in his heart. Neither honor nor manliness had ever stood between him and his fatal passion. Nothing, he thought, no claim of man or child or God, could stop him. No situation had ever before arisen with the power to make him even think of resisting. A million times sweeter sang his nightingale, imperiously, wonderfully. He was in a swift, golden dream, with the thick fragrance of wine, and the dark, mocking, luring eyes on him. All this that was more than life to him—to give it up—to risk it—to put it off an hour! He felt the wrenching pang of something deep hidden in his soul, beating its way up, torturing him. But it was strange and mighty. In that terrible moment it decided for him; and the smile of a child was stronger than the unquenchable and blasting fire of his heart.

Monty untied his saddle and threw it aside; and then with tight-shut jaw he rode down the steep descent to the level valley. His horse was big and strong and fast. He was fresh, too, and in superb condition. Once down on the hard-packed road he broke into a run, and it took an iron arm to hold him from extending himself. Monty calculated on saving the horse for the run back. He had no doubt that would be a race with fire. And he had been in forest fires more than once.

The big bay settled into a steady, easy-running gait. The valley floor sloped up quite perceptibly, and the road was many times cut and crossed by a dry wash. Soon Monty reached the bleached and scraggy cedars— and the scant thickets of scrub oak—and then the straggling pines. They were dwarfed and gnarled, and many were dead. As he advanced, however, these trees grew thicker and larger. Then he rode out of the pines into a park, where the white grass and the gray sage waved in the wind.

A dry, odorous scent of burning wood came on the breeze. He could still see part of the smoke cloud that had alarmed him, but, presently, when he had crossed into the pines again it passed from his sight. The ascent of the valley merged into a level and the slopes widened out and the road crossed park after park, all girdled by pines. Then he entered the forest proper. It was dark and shady. The great pines stood far apart, with only dead limbs low down, and high above, the green, lacy foliage massed together. There was no underbrush. Here and there a fallen monarch lay with great slabs of bark splitting off. The ground was a thick brown mat of pine needles, as dry as powder.

The dry, strong smell of pine was almost sickening. It rushed at Monty—filling his nostrils. And in the treetops there was a steady, even roar of wind. Monty had a thought of how that beautiful brown and green forest, with its stately pines and sunny glades, would be changed in less than an hour.

There seemed to be a blue haze veiling the aisles of the forest, and Monty kept imagining it was smoke. And he imagined the roar in the pines grew louder. It was his impatience and anxiety that made the ride seem so long. But he was immensely relieved when he reached Muncie's corral. It was full of horses, and they were snorting, stamping, heads up, facing the direction of the wind. That wind seemed stronger, more of a warm, pine-laden blast, which smelled of fire and smoke. It appeared to be full of fine dust or ashes. Monty dismounted and had a look at his horse. He was wet and hot, just right for a grueling race. Monty meant to let down the bars of the corral gate, so that Muncie's horses could escape, but he was deterred by the thought that he might need another mount. Then he hurried on to Muncie's cabin.

This was a structure of logs and clapboards, standing in a little clearing, with the great pines towering all around. Presently Monty saw the child, little Del, playing in the yard with a dog. He called. The child heard and being frightened ran into the cabin. The dog came barking toward Monty. He was a big, savage animal, a trained watchdog. But he recognized Monty.

Hurrying forward Monty went to the open door and called Mrs. Muncie. There was no immediate response. He called again. And while he stood there waiting, listening above the roar of the wind he heard a low, dull, thundering sound, like a waterfall in a flooded river. It sent the blood rushing back to his heart, leaving him cold. He had not a single instant to lose.

"Mrs. Muncie," he called louder. "Come out! Bring the child! It's Monty Price. There's forest fire! Hurry!"

Still he did not get an answer. Then he called little Del, with like result. He reflected that the mother had often drove to town, leaving the child in care of the watchdog. Besides, usually Muncie or one of his men was near at hand. But now there did not seem to be anybody here. And that dull, continuous sound shook Monty's nerve. He yelled into the open door. Then he stepped in. There was no one in the big room—or the kitchen. He grew hurried now. The child was hiding. Finally he found her in the clothespress, and he pulled her out. She was frightened. She did not recognize him.

"Del, is your mother home?" he asked.

The child shook her head.

With that Monty picked her up, along with a heavy shawl he saw, and hurrying out, ran down to the corral. The horses were badly frightened now. Monty set little Del down, threw the shawl into a water trough and then he let down the bars of the gate. The horses pounded out in a cloud of dust. Monty's horse was frightened, too, and almost broke away. There was now a growing roar on the wind. It seemed right upon him. Yet he could not see any fire or smoke. The dog came to him, whining and sniffing.

With swift hands Monty soaked the shawl thoroughly in the water, and then wrapping it round little Del and holding her tight, he mounted. The horse plunged and broke and plunged again—then leaped out straight and fast down the road. And Monty's ears seemed pierced and filled by a terrible, thundering roar.

For an instant the awful and unknown sound froze him, stiffened him in his saddle, robbed him of strength. It was the feel of the child that counteracted this and then roused the daredevil in him. The years of his range life had engendered wildness and violence, which now were to have expression in a way new to him.

He had to race with fire. He had to beat the wind of flame to the open parks. Ten miles of dry forest, like powder! Though he had never seen it, he knew fire backed by a heavy wind could rage through dry pine faster than a horse could run. He would fail in the one good deed of his life. And flashing into his mind came the shame and calumny that before had never affected him. It was not for such as he to have the happiness of saving a child. He had accepted a fatal chance; he had forfeited that which made life significant to attempt the impossible. Fate had given him a bitter part to play. But he swore a grim and ghastly oath that he would beat this game. The intense and abnormal passion of the man, damned for years, never controlled, burst within him—and suddenly, terribly, he awoke to a wild joy in this race with fire. He had no love of life—no fear of death. All that he wanted to do—the last thing he wanted to do was to save this child. And to do that he would have burned there in the forest and for a million years in the dark beyond.

So it was with wild joy and rage that Monty Price welcomed this race. He goaded the horse. Then he looked back.

Through the aisles of the forest he saw a strange streaky, murky something, moving, alive, shifting up and down, never an instant the same. It must have been the wind, the heat before the fire. He seemed to see through it, but there was nothing beyond, only opaque, dim, mustering clouds. Hot puffs shot into his face. His eyes smarted and stung. His ears hurt, and were being stopped up. The deafening roar was the roar of avalanches, of maelstroms, of rushing seas, of the wreck and ruin and end of the world. It grew to be so great a roar that he no longer heard. There was only silence. His horse stretched low on a dead run; the tips of the pines were bending in the wind; and wildfire was blowing through the forest, but there was no sound.

Ahead of him, down the road, low under the spreading trees, floated swiftly some kind of a medium, like a transparent veil. It was neither smoke nor air. It carried faint pin points of light, sparks, that resembled atoms of dust floating in sunlight. It was a wave of heat propelled before the storm of fire. Monty did not feel pain, but he seemed to be drying up, parching. All was so strange and unreal—the swift flight between the pines, now growing ghostly in the dimming light—the sense of rushing, overpowering force—and yet absolute silence. But that light burden against his breast—the child—was not unreal.

He fought the desire to look back, but he could not resist it. Some horrible fascination compelled him to look. All behind had changed. A hot wind, like a blast from a furnace blew light, stinging particles into his face. The fire was racing in the treetops, while below all was yet clear. A lashing, leaping, streaming flame engulfed the canopy of pines. It seemed white, seething, inconceivably swift, with a thousand flashing tongues. It traveled ahead of smoke. It was so thin he could see the branches through it and the dirty, fiery clouds behind. It swept onward, a sublime and an appalling spectacle. Monty could not think of what it looked like. It was fire, liberated, freed from the bowels of the earth, tremendous, devouring. This, then, was the meaning of fire. This, then, was the burning of the world.

He must have been insane, he thought, not to be overcome in spirit. But he was not. He felt loss of something, some kind of sensation he ought to have had. But he rode that race keener and better than any race he had ever before ridden. He had but to keep his saddle—to dodge the snags of the trees—to guide the maddened horse. No horse ever in the world had run so magnificent a race. He was outracing the wind and fire. But he was running in terror. For miles he held that long, swift, tremendous stride without a break. He was running to his death whether he distanced the fire or not. For nothing could stop him now except a bursting heart. Already he was blind, Monty thought.

And then, it appeared to Monty, although his steed kept fleeting on faster and faster, that the wind of flame was gaining. The air was too thick to breathe. It seemed ponderous—not from above, but from behind. It had irresistible weight. It pushed Monty and his horse forward in their flight—straws on the crest of a cyclone.

Again he looked back and again the spectacle was different. There was a white and golden fury of flame above, beautiful and binding; and below, farther back, a hellishly dark and glowing fire, black-streaked, with tumbling puffs and streams of yellow smoke. The aisles between the burning pines were smoky, murky caverns, moving, coalescing, weird, and mutable. Monty saw fire shoot from the treetops down the trunks, as if they were trains of powder; and he saw fire shoot up the trunks. They went off like rockets. And along the ground leaped the little flames, like oncoming waves in the surf. He gazed till his eyes burned and blurred, till all merged into a wide, pursuing storm too awful for the gaze of man.

Ahead there was light through the forest. He made out a white, open space of grass. A park! And the horse, like a demon, hurtled onward, with his smoothness of action gone, beginning to break.

A wave of wind, blasting in its heat, like a blanket of fire, rolled over Monty. He saw the lashing tongues of flame above him in the pines. The storm had caught him. It forged ahead. He was riding under a canopy of fire. Burning pine cones, like torches, dropped all around him, upon him. A terrible blank sense of weight, of agony, of suffocation—of the air turning to fire! He was drooping, withering when he flashed from the pine out into an open park. The horse broke and plunged and went down, reeking, white, in convulsions, killed on his feet. There was fire in his mane. Monty fell with him, and lay in the grass, the child in his arms. There was smoke streaming above him, and his ears seemed to wake to a terrible, receding roar. It lessened, passed away, leaving behind a crackling, snapping, ripping sound. The wind of flame had gone on. Monty lay there partially recovering. The air was clearer. Still he was dazed.

Fire in the grass—fire at his legs roused him. He experienced a stinging pain. It revived him. He got up. The park was burning over. It was enveloped in a pall of smoke. But he could see. Drawing back a fold of the wet shawl he looked at the child. She appeared unharmed. Then he set off running away from the edge of the forest. It was a big park, miles wide. Near the middle there was bare ground. He recognized the place, got his bearings, and made for the point where a deep ravine headed out of this park.

Beyond the bare circle there was more fire, burning sage and grass. His feet were blistered through his boots, and then it seemed he walked on redhot coals. His clothes caught fire, and he beat it out with bare hands.

Zane Grey listening for hounds working below the Tonto Rim. This is the country where Monty Price dreamed of his nightingale.

Agony of thirst tortured him, and the beating, throbbing, excruciating pain of burns. He lost his way, but he kept on. And all about him was a chaos of smoke. Unendurable heat drove him back when he wandered near the edge of the pines.

Then he stumbled into the rocky ravine. Smoke and blaze above him—the rocks hot—the air suffocating—it was all unendurable. But he kept on. He plunged down, always saving the child when he fell. His sight grew red. Then it grew dark. All was black, or else night had come. He was losing all pain, all sense when he stumbled into water. That saved him. He stayed there. A long time passed till it was light again. His eyes had a thick film over them. Sometimes he could not see at all. But when he could, he kept on walking, on and on. The weight of the child bore him down. He rested, went on again till all sense, except a dim sight, failed him. Through that, as in a dream, he saw moving figures, men looming up in the gray fog, hurrying to him.

Far south of the Tonto Range, under the purple shadows of the Peloncillos, there lived a big-hearted rancher with whom Monty Price found a home. He did little odd jobs about the ranch that by courtesy might have been called work. He would never ride a horse again. Monty's legs were warped, his feet hobbled. He did not have free use of his hands. And seldom or never in the presence of any one did he remove his sombrero. For there was not a hair on his head. His face was dark, almost black, with terrible scars. A burned-out, hobble-footed wreck of a cowboy! But, strangely, there were those at the ranch who loved him. They knew his story.

VANISHING AMERICA*

by

Zane Grey

. . . My work has been wholly concerned with the beauty and wildness and nature of America, *all of which are vanishing.* . . . I see only one possibility of preserving the game and fish, and something of the natural beauty of wild places, and the purity of inland waters. And here it is. If a million outdoor men who have sons, will think of these sons, and band together to influence other men who have sons—*then we may save something of America's outdoor joys for the boys.* . . .

My appeal is not to save game and fish for sportsmen. I have forgotten sportsmen. I do not care anything about saving game and fish for sportsmen. I want to save something of vanishing America. For its own sake! So that our children's children will know what a fish looks like, and will hear the sweet call of "Bob White;" *and see all the living and nesting inhabitants of our beautiful land.*

We must stand powerfully and unalterably for the future sons of America. Otherwise we will fail of our opportunity. . . . It is a serious thing for any writer to take up his pen against so-called sportsmen, and their peculiar ways of being happy. But it is necessary that this should be done. If honest and direct appeal fails to win thoughtless and ignorant hunters and fishermen to our cause then they must be scorned and flayed and ostracized until they are ashamed of their selfishness. No such

*This text is from an editorial in the second issue of the *Izaak Walton League Monthly*—Volume I, Number 2, September, 1922—the crusading conservation periodical that would soon be retitled *Outdoor America*. If, by the standards prevailing more than half a century later, Zane Grey's exclusively male entreaty in behalf of fathers and sons seems archaically chauvinistic, his concern for a vanishing America is at least as relevant today as it was in 1922. Now as then, a strong argument can be made for the need to persuade every parent that our natural legacy is being squandered, and ours is the responsibility to save it—for our children and our children's children.

appeal, however, can touch the heart of the hardened automobiling sportsmen or the harpooning anglers or the fakirs and would-bes who want to see their pictures and names in newspapers and magazines.

Naturalists and biologists and true lovers of nature either despise or disapprove of sportsmen. There is justice in this. Something is wrong. Our heritage of outdoor pursuits is certainly a noble and splendid thing. Manly endeavor and toil and endurance makes for the progress of the race. Nature abhors weaklings. And red-blooded pursuits operate against the appalling degeneracy of modern days. Nevertheless sportsmen, as a mass, are hypocrites, *and are blind to the hand-writing on the wall.*

My one hope for conservation of American forests and waters is to plant into every American father these queries. Do you want to preserve something of America for your son? Do you want him to inherit something of the love of outdoors that made our pioneers such great men? Do you want him to be manly, strong, truthful, and brave? Do you want him to be healthy? Do you want him, when he grows to manhood, *to scorn his father and nation for permitting the wanton destruction of our forests and the depletion of our waters?*

In this materialistic day it is almost impossible to get the ear of any man. With all men it is the selfish zest of the battle of life. But men do love their sons, and through them perhaps can be reached before it is too late. *The mighty and unquenchable spirit of a million fathers could accomplish much.*

Zane Grey